WILD HORSE COUNTRY IN WYOMING

JACK PRICE

Wild Horse Country in Wyoming

Copyright © 1996 by
Jack Price

First Printing 1996
Second Printing 1997
Third Printing 2000
Fourth Printing 2006

LCCN: 96-93047
ISBN: 1-57579-049-1 (Paperback)
ISBN: 1-57579-050-5 (Hardcover)

Printed in the United States of America
PINE HILL PRESS
4000 West 57th Street
Sioux Falls, SD 57106

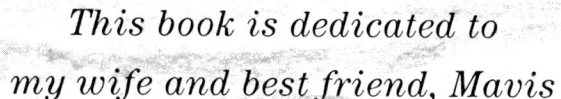

*This book is dedicated to
my wife and best friend, Mavis*

Jack

Acknowledgements

I have written this true story for my kids. I didn't take the time to tell them, while they were growing up, about my exciting times of running wild horses and trapping coyotes as a young lad in Wyoming.

Driven from the plains of South Dakota by drought and dust storms we, the Jake Price Family, found a refuge in the sage brush and cedar covered hills of Wyoming.

My special thanks to Rita who typed the original manuscript, Karma for the sketch of Boar's Tusk, Jerry and Kathy for typing and committing this to a word processor, Mrs. Frank Robbins, and Bill Logan Jr. for many of the pictures, and family members for pictures and other materials.

Thanks also to my wife Mavis, who never complains about my room full of photos, clippings, memorabilia and other things sometimes known as junk.

Table of Contents

The Decision to Move

The year was 1937. I had just completed the 6th grade at Nunda, SD public school. It seemed like rain was a thing of the past. All we could seem to get was bad electrical storms and wind that turned the dust filled air nearly as dark as night. Motorists drove with their lights on in the middle of the day when the wind blew.

We wished for Dad to be home, but he had gone to Wyoming with Ben Brunie and Blackie Bonnin to look for bucking stock to add to what we had.

Dad had farmed and traded horses until all the crops dried up and blew away. He would buy several Model T Fords and take them west of the Missouri River. The Indians welcomed the chance to trade horses for the Fords. He would come home trailing a bunch of broncs and driving a pair on his covered wagon that he took along as living quarters.

After he got them home, there would be exciting times as Dad and my older brothers would break the biggest ones to work in the harness. The smaller ones were broke for saddle horses. Occasionally, one would be bad enough to use in the bucking string that he was gradually building. These western horses were usually smaller than the general run of work horses but they were tough, and farmers liked them when they got used to them.

Farmers would usually have an old or crippled horse they would trade for the broncs and pay a little to boot. Dad would keep the old ones until he had a railroad carload of them. Then he would ship them off to a fox farm to be used as fox feed. This too had died off real bad with the drought and depression. Having been a rodeo cowboy in his younger years, he had turned to producing rodeos. He had gradually worked over into Minnesota where money wasn't quite as scarce.

I had gotten a taste of riding in the rodeos. Calves were my specialty, but I did tackle a big old Brahma bull with only one horn. The plan was, I'd ride him out quite a ways from the chute and a pickup man would pick me off because the bull was big and it would be a long ways to fall. I had a sharp pair of spurs and decided I was quite a cowboy, so I put the spurs to him in the shoulders. Consequently, he lost me on about the fourth jump. I got up and dusted myself off. Nothing was hurt but my pride and that was quick to heal.

We hadn't thought much of it when Dad left for Wyoming because he had been gone a lot anyway. The excitement started when he returned home about ten o'clock one night and called everyone together. I was in bed but it didn't take long for me to join the family circle. After we had all arrived and had a hug by our loving father, he proceeded to tell us about his trip to Wyoming. they had gone to Rock Springs and then south past Firehole and down to Trout Creek to Jim Ramsay's ranch. Blackie Bonnin was an Indian and had been all over that country before. It was ideal ranch country with pine covered mountains and cedar covered hills. There were snow fed streams and springs so there was plenty of water for livestock and wild game. Firehole had plenty of wild horses, free if you could catch them.

Dad had really taken a liking to Wyoming and had made arrangements for us to move out there. Mother wasn't so sure, but dad assured her that there was work out there and with eight kids to feed, it was quite necessary to be where he could make a living. My older brothers were old enough to work out too, but it had been real hard for them to get more than part time work in South Dakota.

The next few weeks went by pretty slow for me. I could hardly wait to get started west. To me this was like a dream come true. Most of my time was spent telling my friends about where we were going and that we would probably be running wild horses. Some of them seemed somewhat envious and I even promised a few wild horses to my closest friends. At twelve years old this didn't seem to be any problem to me. The fact that it was nearly 900 miles out there became a reality to me later.

This was a busy time for Dad, Mother, and my older brothers. They had to decide what we could take along and what we would have to sell. We would be taking a 1929 four door Chevrolet with a two wheeled trailer behind. Everything that we took would be hauled in or tied on this two piece vehicle. I can remember Mother saying she wouldn't give up her washing machine. She had just gotten a new Speed Queen with a Briggs and Stratton engine on it. Nor would she give up her sewing machine. It was a Singer treadle machine that she had gotten from Grandma Glaze. These were considered necessities of course, and were the first things to go into the trailer. There was one thing that I had become very attached to and it hit me pretty hard when I realized that he would have to be sold. This was "Jack," a little brown mule that Dad had brought home to us kids about a year earlier.

When questioned about the name, I'd always say, "He was named that when we got him and it's also my name and neither of us wants to change it." He was a little bit of a mule, about the size of a big Shetland Pony. We could drive him or ride him. We could hook him onto anything. He'd try to pull it but if he couldn't he'd just stand there. If he could pull it, away we'd go. He wasn't afraid of anything. When we rode him, he neck reined and was just as good as any cow pony. He wouldn't carry double though. If two of us got on, he'd pitch us right off. He was a little hard to stay on anyway because Mules' withers aren't as high as horses. I had used him on one section of harrow to drag the garden after it had been plowed in the spring. We had worked hard planting a garden just to have it dry up and blow away. We found a good home for Jack, a family very much like our own. I don't know what Dad got for him, if anything. The main thing was that he had a good home.

We had another family pet. He was a black and tan coon hound named Prince. Dad said he'd come in handy for trailing bobcats and badgers in Wyoming, so he built a box on the left running board of the Chevrolet for him to ride in.

Our sale went very poorly. We didn't have a lot of good machinery and household goods anyway, but there wasn't much money in the country and people weren't buying. I remember our clamp-on ice skates sold for 5 cents a pair. Some of the furniture was sold to Guy Wood who ran a second hand store in town. I remember later, Mother saying she had left all of our birth certificates in a glass fronted desk that she sold to him.

The time finally came for us to load up and leave. We were really loaded down with a trailer load behind and a tent rolled up full of bedding on top of the car. On the very top of the trailer we had three saddles. We had Dad, Mom, Chuck, Short, Marcy, Rosie, Me, Sweed, and Jean in the car, and a coon hound in a box on the running board. My second brother, Don, was working in Minnesota and would join us in Wyoming later.

We pulled out of Nunda in the dark. I would guess about 4 o'clock in the morning. We were supposed to try to get some sleep in the car but I was too excited to sleep. We seemed to roll along at a pretty good clip all forenoon, stopping once in awhile to check things over. The trailer had wooden spoke wheels and Dad was concerned about the heavy load on them. But, the wheels were the least of our problems. It must have been about noon, I was riding in the seat directly behind Dad, who was driving, when it seemed like we passed behind a big grove of trees. The shadow passed over the car and the next thing I knew I was regaining consciousness lying in the road ditch alongside the car. Dad was fanning me with his cowboy hat that he always wore. About two minutes after I came to, Dad keeled over. He too, had been overcome with carbon monoxide gas. He wasn't out very long, but we were both very sick, about the same as having a bad case of the flu, only worse. We were close to Freeman, South Dakota so we drove there with our windows open.

They couldn't work on the exhaust system until the next morning so we went out of town about a mile and set our tent up in somebody's pasture. The garage had it fixed by mid-afternoon the next day and we continued on our way. We were already a day late for our rendezvous with the Monty Barber family who we were supposed to meet at the south end of the bridge at Yankton. They were coming from Sioux Falls and would be traveling with us to Wyoming. Just after we crossed the bridge into Nebraska, we came to a little natural park where the Barbers had set up camp and were waiting patiently for our arrival.

Monty Barber was younger than Dad, a good bronc rider and trick roper. He did rope spinning tricks as good as I've ever seen. His family consisted of his wife, Helen, his son, Monty Dale, 5 years old and his daughter, Joane, 3 years old. They had a dog too.

Monty had a big Packard, about a 1927, but in real good shape. His wife also had brought her sewing machine which sat very easily between the front seat and the rear seat. They didn't have a trailer to pull but had their car loaded down pretty good.

It was almost sundown by the time we joined the Barbers so we set up camp for the night. There was much visiting and laughter around the campfire that night but I hardly enjoyed it because I was still sick from the gas.

My oldest brother, Chuck, and I shared a bed under the stars that night. Dad was up at the crack of dawn the next morning waking everybody up. After a campfire breakfast, we packed up our camping gear and headed out. Let me tell you that Nebraska is one long state. We traveled on US 30 which has since been replaced by I-80.

The trip across was uneventful but everyone gave a loud cheer when we reached a big roadside sign which said "Welcome to Wonderful Wyoming." Our first night in Wyoming was spent just east of Cheyenne. The next night was spent at a place called Piker Springs just west of Rawlins. I remember this place. There was a gas station and the place had a toilet with the roof blown off. Somebody took a picture of Dad as he stood up after finishing his morning toiletries.

The next day, after stopping in Rock Springs for a few necessities, we headed out to the south country where we were to make our new home. It was a dirt road that had been dozed out of the sage brush and rocks. It was rough and dusty, to say the least.

We passed by Songster's Coal Mine where they still used mules to haul the coal to the surface from inside the mine. We followed the road and it led up Little Bitter Creek until we came to Bacon Hill. We stopped at the spring at the bottom of the hill and all had a taste of real spring water. Bacon Hill proved to be too much for the old Chevrolet with it's heavy load. She couldn't pull the hill. We loaded everybody that could squeeze into Barber's car and drove on. Dad and the other kids stayed with the stalled outfit after telling Monty how to get to the closest ranch that he knew of. The first ranch was Bill Logan's but the only one home was Mrs. Logan. The rest were out looking for her brother Jack Teeters who had been lost for about three days. She directed us to Grover Logan's place only about a mile farther up Trout Creek.

By this time, it was really dark and the surrounding cedar covered hills seemed like mountains to us. Mother was pretty upset at the thought of a grown man who was familiar with the country being lost. I suppose she had visions of us kids scattering in every direction and she'd never see us again.

The Logans were very nice to us. Grover and Monty took Logans truck and went back and pulled our over-burdened Chevrolet up the hill. By the time they returned, Lila Logan, with the help of Mother and Helen Barber, had prepared a good home cooked meal which we all enjoyed very much. We pitched our tent in their yard that night.

The Logans had a son, Jack, a year older than I, and a daughter, Marjorie, a couple of years younger. We had a real good getting acquainted visit that night. Jack and I hit it off good right from the start. He showed me where we would go to school in just a few short weeks. It was a room that had originally been part of their house.

Grover was a Federal Government trapper who was hired to keep the coyote population down. Every spring while the coyotes were having pups, he would be gone for about two weeks with a saddle horse and a pack horse out in the territory assigned to him. He found the dens and destroyed the pups. It seemed like a cruel job but as we sat outside the log house on this clear night we could hear many coyotes howling. I figured one man in this big county couldn't possibly get them all.

The next morning we all slept later than usual, knowing that we were only a mile and a half from our destination. The morning was nothing less than beautiful as we topped the last hill and we looked down upon the green meadows and the few scattered buildings of log. This was the McGath place and was to be our new home. I couldn't have been happier if we had been rich. We were far from that though because I heard Dad tell Mom that he only had 50 cents left after he had bought the groceries in Rock Springs.

This trip really showed the pioneer blood in my dad and my frail little mother who didn't weigh 100 pounds soaking wet.

The next few days were spent getting settled. The main house had only two big rooms. There was a smaller log building that Barbers moved into. We were all pretty cramped but we didn't mind because we were always a togetherness family. Across the creek was a barn and set of corrals.

On about the third day, Jimmy and Wanda Ramsay came riding into the yard. They were riding bare back. They explained that they had been looking for Jack Teeters and had left their saddles in somebody's truck and they hadn't returned them yet. Jack had found himself, eventually, riding into territory familiar to him. Wanda was my age but taller and had a boyish bob haircut. Jim was a couple of years younger. They stayed until almost sundown and we had a good visit. They told about a lot of experiences they had on the ranch and we told them all about our trip out to Wyoming from South Dakota.

There were deer on the meadow nearly every night so we had meat on the table. Lila Logan had evidently had a good rutabaga and turnip crop which she shared liberally with us. We had always heard that porcupine was good to eat so we decided to try it. One evening just before dark, I saw one on the meadow west of the house. Dad let me take the 410 shotgun and go after it. He only gave me one shell because he said I could get real close to it. Even though I did get real close, somehow I missed him. Having decided not to go back without the meat, I clobbered it with the stock of the gun. This was the wrong thing to do because it broke the stock. I went back to the house feeling pretty sheepish about the gun, but I did have the porcupine. Dad dressed it out and we had it for supper the next night. It was fatty like pork and tasted similar to pork, but not much of it got eaten. I'm sure it was the thought of what kind of animal it was more than the taste that kept us from eating it.

Dad had bought three saddle horses when he'd gone to Wyoming the first time. One was a tall white horse named Whitey. One was a bob-tailed bay named Bob and one was a buckskin named Buck. They were all gentle horses but old Whitey was the one us kids rode most. He was lazy but could jump out of any corral that he didn't want to be in. Short rode him to the Jarvie Ranch about 20 miles away. He had gone over there looking for work. It got late so he stayed all night. The next morning old Whitey was gone so Short had to borrow a horse to ride home. Tom Jarvie told Short to turn his horse loose when he got home. He knew he would return to the ranch. Old Whitey showed up at home about sundown looking for oats. Mother was a little upset thinking that he might have thrown short off. We always thought she did a lot of unnecessary worrying, but isn't that just like a mother?

The summer slipped away very swiftly and soon we were hiking off to school. The teacher was Mrs. Boyer. I always felt that she didn't have enough patience to be a teacher. If we couldn't get something through our head she was always nearby to pound it in with a pencil, a book or anything handy. She was working on Sweed one day and I told her she had better leave him alone. She said "If you don't like the way I run this school you can leave." So I got up and went home. My mother hit the ceiling when I got home and told her what had happened. The next morning she said "You go back to school and keep your mouth shut." This is exactly what I did and had very little trouble after that.

Marcy, who was out of school, would come after us kids on old Whitey once in awhile. We were always happy for a ride home from school, so we would all five pile on him with me in the very rumble seat. It never failed that I would slide off his tail end as we climbed the hill by the "sheep keep off gate." This was a gate in a boundary fence that had been set up to keep sheep off the land owned privately by cattle ranchers. It

Pupils of Maxon School 1936—1 year before we came.
L to R back: Wanda Ramsay, Milan Bonnon, Bill Logan Jr. 2nd row: Marjorie
Logan, Jack Logan, Jim Ramsay. Front. Roy Logan.

was old and broken down, probably built at the time of the range wars between sheep men and cattle men.

Mrs. Boyer smoked cigarettes, which was very uncommon for a woman in that time period. Consequently, she tried to hide the fact by smoking in the toilet. Now this old out house was used by all. There were no separate buildings for boys or girls or for the Logan family.

We boys were instructed to go behind the toilet to do #1, obviously to keep the seat dry. If you were next to use it after the teacher, you could hardly breathe from inhaling her smoke. This prompted us to smoke her out of the school room. Jack Logan said "If she likes smoke so well, we will smoke her out." With that, he grabbed a cardboard box and proceeded to the roof with it. The box fit perfectly and snugly over the chimney. By the time classes were reconvened, the stove was beginning to issue out short bursts of smoke, causing much coughing, sneezing and a few teary eyes. Most of these symptoms were exaggerated because the kids were all in on the gag, but Mrs. Boyer couldn't imagine why the stove had all of a sudden gone into smoking convulsions.

School was out early that day and we Price kids went home before someone would have time to discover the box and ruin the whole plan. I'm sure Jack waited for a chance when he wouldn't be seen to go up to remove the box. The stove worked fine from then on. I doubt if Mrs. Boyer ever found out what caused the smoking stove.

Jim's Little Gray...and PeeWee

We had lived at the McGath place for about two months before I had a chance to see Jim's "Little Gray." Jim and Wanda often talked about him. They had learned to ride and rope on him and a little sorrel, bald faced stocking legged horse named Sample.

The little gray was a small horse, probably weighed 650 or 700 pounds. He was a slim, fine boned horse and could run like the wind in his prime. With a light rider on his back, he could do almost anything that a horse weighing 1200 pounds could do.

One evening after school I went home with Jim to spend the evening. We went right to the stack yard where the little horse was eating alfalfa leaves. He had the run of the ranch because his teeth were about worn out and he was allowed to graze where he could get the best food available.

Jim got a hand full of oats and called the retired pony over to the fence where we fed the treat of oats to him. He nickered as he approached us, definitely expecting a treat of some kind. Occasionally Jim slipped him an apple. Candy was out because his teeth were bad enough already. He was in good shape, with a sleek and shiny coat of hair. He frisked about as Jim pretended to try to catch him. It was easy to see he was enjoying his retirement.

Jim had gotten a little Appaloosa gelding from Brick Williams to take the place of the little gray. The Appaloosa, named PEEWEE was a small horse too, but bigger than the gray.

This relieved the little gray of most of his duties, but he was still called upon occasionally to give rides to very small cowboys and cowgirls who visited the ranch. They surely enjoyed the old pony and he seemed to enjoy having the kids around for him to give rides to. This went on until the little

11

gray was called to graze upon the lush green grass of Cayuse Heaven.

Jimmy Ramsay rode hard every morning on his way to school, at least as far as our place where he rode slowly and we visited as we Price kids walked to school.

One morning Jim had ol' PEEWEE all stretched out looking like he was heading for the home stretch. They were coming through the bull pasture, as usual but what he didn't know was that his Dad had been down there earlier to close the gate so he could turn the bulls out into the pasture.

Sweed, Jean and I were just leaving the house to go to school when we heard a crash and a thud. We looked to the west just in time to see horse and rider jump up out of a cloud of dust. They had run into the wire gate. Luckily neither one of them was hurt. For a long time after that incident, Jim had a hard time getting old PEEWEE to go through that gate. The little horse didn't want anything like that happening again.

Time dragged on for us at the Maxon School, with only nine kids in the whole school, we couldn't have much of a line up for a ball game and that was about the only kind of recreation equipment we had. We would play hide and seek or kick the can, hiding out behind the log buildings of Logan's ranch, or along Trout Creek in the tall thick sage brush. The creek was neither deep, nor wide but it was surely wet and cold. Occasionally somebody would fall in as they attempted a hurried crossing on their way to the post where they would be in free. This happened to me one day and I was sent home from school. It was a nice warm day with a slight breeze, which had me almost dry by the time I got home.

As fall gave way to winter, a beautiful cover of white snow blanketed the whole countryside.

Dad, Chuck and Don had put together camping gear, several rolls of wire and cable, along with tools for building a corral and headed for Fire Hole, where wild horses were plentiful. They also took along traps for trapping coyotes, badgers and bob cats.

Two razor sharp axes were considered necessities for cutting cedar posts as well as chopping fire wood.

Don had come from Minnesota at Thanksgiving time to be with the Family. He brought along a 38-40 rifle with a hexagon barrel. That thing was a real cannon. He took it out to show me how it would shoot. He shot a cottontail rabbit at about fifty yards. There wasn't enough left of that rabbit to take home. The old gun, which very much resembled a crow bar, had quite a kick to it. Don asked if I wanted to shoot it. I gave it some thought, but used the excuse that we probably should save the ammunition.

Christmas at Horse Camp

Don had come home with the team of horses to get supplies for the horse camp and to take me back with him. I was very happy to get to spend Christmas vacation at the horse camp.

Dad had gotten a long straight pine pole and fastened it to the trailer hitch of the trailer we had brought from South Dakota. This enabled us to hitch a team of horses to it, converting it to a very handy run-about for hauling posts, wire and other supplies.

We had loaded it about 1/2 full of hay which we were glad to have to burrow down into so we could keep warm on our ten mile trip on a winter day.

We started out just after noon, the team was feeling good and started off at a brisk trot. The trailer was light and pulled easy. The tug chains jingled and seemed to play a little tune, as we headed down the canyon towards the Logan ranches. The

Don had come home with the team of horses.

logs rattled as we crossed the Mexican Bridge, named this because it had been built by Mexicans. The structure built of logs and poles spanned a narrow but deep wash.

We didn't stop at either of the Logan ranches, as we had to keep moving if we were to arrive in camp before dark.

As we crossed the bridge over Sage Creek, near Bill Logan's ranch, we could see where Trout Creek empties into Sage Creek, adding to the size of the stream.

Continuing on down the canyon about five miles we passed the Harris place which was owned by the Gottschie Ranches.

The shadows were beginning to grow long and we noticed many mule deer on the meadows.

Not far beyond the Harris place we left the main road to follow a two track road which wasn't much more than two trails side by side. We soon began to climb as the road followed a draw which would eventually end at the top of a big ridge. We followed the ridge (blown bare of snow by the wind) to a thick grove of cedar trees. There, nestled in the cedars was our tent with a good fire burning in the stove within. The aroma of fresh brewed coffee and frying venison reached my cold nose and it relayed the message to my empty stomach. We were soon eating supper and making plans for the following day. The corral needed about a day's work on it before it would be ready. The stove smoked a little because the pipe wasn't big enough in diameter and didn't allow enough draft. This burned my eyes for awhile but I soon crawled into bed and closed them, not to awaken until morning.

I awoke to the sound of Dad slapping on the ceiling of the tent. It was snowing hard outside and sticking to the warm roof of the tent. If it was allowed to build up it could collapse the tent or leak in. It was morning but there was no sign of the sun.

Don and Chuck were outside melting snow in two wash tubs over a fire. The nearest spring was about a mile away so they were melting snow to make water for use at camp.

Sour dough pancakes with Log Cabin syrup was on the breakfast menu. They tasted good on the snowy, cold morning. After breakfast Dad said he, Don and Chuck would take the saddle horses to the spring to water and finish the corral. I should stay in camp where it was warm and dry. I hoped the disappointment didn't show too much, but I was sure anxious to see the corral. After they had been gone for quite a long time I became restless and decided to take a walk and to do a little scouting around on my own. First was the corral where our saddle horses and team were held. This was known by the local folks as the cedar corral. It had been built and used extensively as a wild horse corral. I had asked Dad why we didn't use it to corral wild horses, and he explained that all of the horses for miles around knew where this corral was, and wouldn't go near it if they were being chased.

The old corral was made of whole cedar trees which had been cut with axes and piled in a circle filling in between the standing cedars. There hadn't been very many post holes dug for this wild horse corral. Ralph Reed had built the cedar corral, and I'm sure he had success with it. Others used it because of it's location on a trail, which was a main passage way between Sage Creek and Fire Hole. After having a good look at the cedar corral, I decided to take the 22 rifle to possibly bag a cottontail or a sage chicken, both of these are delicious and at age 12 as fast as I was growing, food occupied a very prominent spot in my every day life.

The 22 Special would be a better gun to carry as it had more power and more range than the plain 22 rifle. The cartridge is larger than the regular 22, but not as large as the 25-20. After checking to make sure it was loaded, I set out heading for the Sage Creek rim which was only about 200 yards away. As I walked among the cedars with the snow beginning to come down harder I watched for some sign of game. One cottontail scurried off into the trees before I could draw a bead on it. When I finally walked out of the trees expecting to look over the rim into Sage Creek, and familiar territory, what a surprise I had! Before me was territory strange to me! There stood a tall natural rock chimney. This would be what the old timers called Maggie's nipple. Dad and the boys had talked about this but I didn't know it was so close to the camp. Coming out on the wrong side of the ridge messed up my sense of direction so I didn't really know which way our camp was. After walking for about 10 minutes, in a direction which proved to be wrong, I decided to back track before my tracks became completely covered with the rapidly falling snow. The camp sure looked good to me as I stepped out into the clearing. I spent the rest of the day getting dried out and warm again.

The snowy day was followed by sunshine, much to our pleasure. After breakfast we all saddled up and rode towards the corral. Whitey was my steed for the day, a good gentle horse a little on the lazy side, but I got along with him pretty well. We continued eastward across the top which gently sloped to the east for about three quarters of a mile where it abruptly dropped off into Fire Hole.

Dad rode Bob, the bob-tailed bay, Don rode Buck and Chuck was on Skeeter, a horse that belonged to Ramsays.

Dad gave us the plan as we rode across the flat. He and Chuck would ride down the ridge to spot a herd of wild horses which they would try to bring up the ridge to where Don would turn them down the draw with the corral in it. I was stationed over the edge of the ridge on a well used horse trail. My job was to be where I could see the ridge, and still be out of sight of any horses which came up it. If the horses started down the trail I was sitting on, I would show up to turn them up the ridge towards Don, I was to keep out of sight. I built a small fire out of some dry cedar sticks. I could be in for a long wait.

The dry cedar snapped and crackled as the flames reached lazily towards the sky. the smoke was light, appearing to be almost transparent as it also made it's way heavenward on this calm winter day.

I couldn't see Don from where I was, and it wasn't necessary that I see him as long as I knew where he was stationed. My assurance of this came through a small bunch of antelope which watched him from a distance. They spooked a couple of times which made me think they would probably leave the area. They continued to graze, watching Don out of the corner of their eyes. They had evidently found a good spot to feed and weren't too willing to give it up.

As I sat on a clump of sage brush in the comfort of the little fire, my mind wandered back a few years. It was Christmas vacation also, but it was definitely a colder day then, with a breeze blowing from the northwest. Don had taken me with him to look at his traps. I had dressed warm enough and even though I was only six years old, I had no doubt that I would have a good time following my older brother.

Don was always a hunter, fisherman and trapper. We always said he could smell in a hole and tell if it was occupied by some wild animal. This was a kind of tongue in cheek expression, but he could tell in a short while if a hole was being used, and by what kind of animal.

On that cold December day in South Dakota I had a very chilling experience.

We had walked about a quarter of a mile following the little creek which ran past our house on the Hilstead farm, near the Jim river. Don had walked somewhat faster than I and was probably 25 yds. ahead of me, when he jumped the creek. Being pre-occupied with his trap line, he failed to warn me about the springs in the creek causing the ice to remain thin. As I stepped onto the ice I felt it give way and heard it crack. I let out a yell just before I went through the ice where the water was over my head.

Don was there in an instant to haul me out of the icy water and into the frigid air. He took me by the hand and we headed for the house.

That was a long trip for me as I was soaking wet and getting colder by the minute. By the time we arrived at the door my clothes were getting frozen stiff. I was lucky we were no farther from the house than we were.

A running buck antelope brought me back to the present. He was soon followed by a bunch of fast moving horses. Bringing up the rear was Dad on the bob-tailed bay who was running well, keeping up with the wild ones.

As Dad rode by, he motioned for me to follow so I would be there to help corral the horses if Don could get them headed down the right trail.

Don was watching and mounted up, expecting the wild horses to turn down the trail leading to the corral. the horses had a different idea. As Don rode out trying to turn them, they split and went on both sides of him, later joining to run down the ridge just beyond the draw which lead to the corral.

Don took the rope from the strap on the pommel of the saddle, built a loop and soon singled out a nice bay mare. He dropped right in behind her, swinging the loop. She was sure nervous and kept looking back as she ran. She was getting tired and couldn't get away from the buckskin. Don threw the loop, guiding it nicely over her head. The mare lunged as she hit the end of the rope, giving the buckskin a violent jerk. Old Buck was wise to all the tricks of the trade involved in being a rope horse, so he was braced and ready.

Dad and I soon arrived on the scene to help with the wild mare. With Dad on one side with his rope on her, and Don on the other with his rope on her, and with me behind her, it wasn't too difficult to take her back to the camp.

Chuck had cut across towards camp after running the wild ones for several miles and turning them over to Dad. Skeeter was needing a rest, and with the sun edging ever closer to the horizon, it was evident that another short winter day was about to end.

When we arrived in camp, chuck had a pot of coffee made. This really hit the spot.

The mare was snubbed up close between the two saddle horses while Dad and Don worked slowly and cautiously to put a heavy halter on her. Dad had made this halter of extra heavy leather, for just this purpose. A long thick rope was placed around her flanks. This type of rope doesn't easily burn a horse. the rope was then worked between her front legs, through the halter ring, and tied to a cedar tree. She was left this way for a couple of days, "Fed and watered by hand" until she got the pull out of her system. When she had discovered she couldn't get away, the rope was put around her neck, then through the halter ring and tied to something solid. We were soon leading her to water and she gentled down nicely.

The Price boys at the McGoth place in 1938.
L to R back: Harland "Short," Donald and Charles. Front: Leonard "Jack"
and Elwood "Sweed."

When the excitement was over for the day, and we were
discussing the day's events, Dad said he figured the wild bunch
had known where the corral was. That's why they nearly ran
over Don to get on the next ridge which would by-pass the corral.

The stove, fueled by dry cedar wood, snapped and popped
loudly at times. I could almost believe somebody had thrown a
few rounds of live ammunition into it. the heat was very com-
forting causing me to crawl down between the blankets of the
bedroll where I ended up in dreamland.

That corral in Fire Hole looked like a sure thing for corralling mustangs, built in the bottom of a draw, with horse
trails leading down it. Possibly the trails were too well used
and the horses all knew where it was, but we never did corral
any horses there. The winter wasn't a complete loss, however,
as they set out a trap line and were able to catch many coyotes,

badgers and bob cats. By marketing these in Rock Springs at Wieses and Doanes fur buying companies, they were able to keep the family in groceries and to buy oats for the horses.

Christmas vacation didn't last nearly long enough and it was back to the old grind in school.

Spring came at last and Dad, Chuck and Don went to Rock Springs to look for work. Don got on at the Union Pacific coal mine. Dad and Chuck said they wouldn't work below ground so they looked for ranch work. Chuck hired on with IH Dearth who headquartered in Eden Valley. Dad hired on with Chilton Ranches, who headquartered in Rock Springs.

Cowboys

In my way of thinking, Jim Ramsay and Bill Logan could each be classified as a Cowboy's Cowboy. They had done it all. They could ride and rope with the best, both having grown up in the saddle. They were wise to the ways of the elements involved in ranching in the rugged country of Southwestern Wyoming. The weather was always to be reckoned with in raising livestock and the feed for it.

In their youth they had been lured by the excitement of the rodeo. Each cowboy packed his saddle into a burlap bag, swung it up on a shoulder, and together boarded the Union Pacific train at Rock Springs, destined for Cheyenne Frontier Days. This rodeo was labeled "The Grand Daddy of them all." They rode well in Cheyenne and many other rodeos. Deciding they couldn't run a ranch and be gone so much of the time, they returned to their ranches. Both loved the rodeo experience, but were ranchers at heart and were soon tending their cattle and raising a family.

Bill was married to Rose Teeters. Their children were Bill Jr., Roy, and Steve. Jim was married to Barbra Bates. Their children were Jimmy and Wanda. Jimmy still lives on the ranch, and Wanda is a rancher's wife, living near Graystone, Colorado.

The Logan Ranch was never without activity. One summer I stayed a week with Bill and Roy. There were the usual chores to be done such as milking the cow, gathering eggs and chopping and hauling in fire wood.

Normally they used water from Sage Creek but a heavy rain several miles above the ranch had caused the creek to swell and to get all riled up and muddy. When this happened, the drinking water was hauled in canvas water bags from the Iron Spring. The spring water, bubbling clear and cold from the side of the mountain contained a higher than normal amount

Jim and Barbra Ramsay, 1961.

of iron. This was the reason for the name Iron Spring. The water was very good to drink and it stayed cold in the bags.

Bill, Roy and I rode to the spring, which was about two miles from the ranch, to fill the bags and haul them home. We enjoyed this chore on horse-back. It only lasted for a couple of days until the creek water cleared up again.

Haying on Logan Ranch. Bill Logan Jr. on stack.

It was haying time at Logan's when I was there. Bill Sr. was mowing alfalfa with one team while Bill Jr. was raking with another on the dump rake making long windrows of the partly cured hay by spacing the dumps evenly each time he crossed the field. After the hay laid for a couple of days and was completely cured they used another bucker type implement, called a bull rake, to push the hay onto the stacker teeth. The bull rake was also pulled by horses. After the hay was pushed onto the stacker teeth a truck tied to a long cable pulled it up and dropped it onto the stack. One man with a pitch fork stood on the stack to arrange the hay and shape the stack with a high center and sloping sides to shed water.

I got the job of running the truck. It was just back and forth for the length of the cable but I enjoyed doing it. The old truck ran good. I don't know what kind or what year it was but it had a self starter on it. No doubt it was built in the 1920's.

My many visits at Logans were always pleasurable and this one certainly came to an end too soon.

Logans sold their ranch when Bill and Rose retired and moved to Rock Springs. Bill served as the Sweetwater County brand inspector for many years. The boys have worked and been in business in the Rock Spring area.

Things were never really quiet around the Ramsay Ranch either. A story often told is of the new school mom who had gone out to call on the patrons of the Maxon school, where she would be teaching the following term. She had brought along two of her school mates to help bolster her courage. This school was located thirty five miles from town, over less than good roads.

The girls became fascinated with Mary, Ramsay's pet burro. They asked if she was gentle, which she surely was, but she also was tricky. They asked if they could ride her. The burro's bridle was put on her and all three teachers proceeded to mount up at the same time. Now old Mary was no dummy and after sizing up the situation, she decided this would be an opportune time to have a drink. She trotted right up to the edge of the creek, stopped and dropped her head to drink. You'd think she hadn't had a drink for days. The three school moms landed squealing and screaming in the creek. They were soon out of the water, looking for a sunny place out of the wind to dry off a bit before starting back home.

Alfie Robertson worked in the Union Pacific Coal mines in Rock Springs. He loved to help out at Ramsay's Ranch on his days off. He would be out there helping with round up, haying, irrigating or anything to do with ranching. One time while he was helping with the haying, he gave my brother, Sweed, a ride in his pickup. They had no more than got started, when Alfie drug out the snuff can. After taking a healthy sized pinch for himself, he offered it to Sweed. Being about ten years old and having never tried Copenhagen, Sweed also took a big pinch, tucking it under his lip, just like Alfie had done. This seemed like the manly thing to do. They hadn't gone far when Sweed had to get out and throw up his guts. Alfie liked Sweed and I'm sure he felt sorry for him, but I also believe he knew he was doing him a favor, because Sweed surely wasn't ever bothered with the snuff habit.

Alfie gave Sweed a toy cast iron truck. It was a good sized one with wheels that turned. The stock rack on it had a gate on hinges, allowing it to open and close. We had a lot of fun playing in the sand down by Trout Creek, but we neglected to bring the truck up out of the creek bed at night. One flash flood in the night is all it took to wash it away or possibly it was buried in the sand. We didn't find it after that.

The deep washes were fun to play in but we had to be careful because in places the banks had been under cut by the erosion of swift moving water. These banks came crashing down unexpectedly and would almost certainly mean sure death to anyone under them. We also had to be aware of the weather. A cloud burst on Little Mountain could send a flash flood raging down Trout Creek. These floods came in the form of a huge wall of water which could be heard raging down the channel before it could be seen.

Jim Ramsay had a dam in Trout Creek about a mile above the ranch. From the reservoir formed by the water backed up by the dam through a series of ditches, flowed the water for watering his crops. Alfalfa was his main crop, grown for hay to feed his livestock. He also had a big vegetable garden where much of the food for the ranch was produced.

There were many beaver up in Trout Creek. They too had dams in the creek. Quite often the water would cease to flow down one of the irrigation ditches. Jim would saddle a horse and ride up to the dam. He would usually find a cut in the bank of his ditch where the beavers had evidently decided they were getting the short end of the stick as far as the water supply was concerned.

Jim said the beaver were quite a nuisance but he knew they were good conservationists and didn't mind repairing the ditches they had caused to leak. In later years the Fish and Game Department trapped the beaver out of Trout Creek, much to Jim's disliking. He said it sure cut down on the amount of water the creek produced in late summer.

Jim was a whistler. Wherever he rode or worked he whistled. He could usually be heard whistling, "Red River Valley," or "Moonlight and Shadows," before he could be seen riding down the trail with a shovel over his shoulder, heading for which ever alfalfa meadow was due to be watered on that particular morning.

Anyone riding into the yard of either Ramsay's or Logan's Ranch was asked "When did you eat last?" If it had been awhile, and it usually had been, they were fed as soon as possible. Their horse was cared for with feed and water. If it was after noon, they were just automatically expected to stay the night. This was pretty much the normal custom all over the west. The hospitality was unbeatable. To a large extent, it hasn't changed, but with our modern modes of transportation making even the most remote area accessible, people have had to become a little less open with their hospitality.

Jim Ramsay had lived his whole life on Trout Creek, leaving just long enough to serve his time in the army in World War I. He served in France for a year in the Veterinary Corps. He was a farrier and blacksmith, a trade which he learned and served him well in his ranching career.

On the ranch, he had a well equipped blacksmith shop to work with. It was complete with a forge for heating metal and an anvil on which to pound out the red hot metal. He had most of the tools needed for general maintenance around the ranch, plus the horse shoeing tools.

Jim was preparing to shoe a horse while I was visiting with Jimmy so I had an excellent opportunity to see how he did it. He had the forge going to heat the shoes and was shaping each one so he gave special attention to it. Being fascinated by the forge, I stayed close to Jim where I could watch the whole procedure. He asked if I would turn the crank which ran the blower under the fire pot of the forge. I was happy to help as this was a new way to shoe horses to me. Dad always shod our horses, shaping the foot to fit the shoe. As I turned the crank, being a boy, I had to experiment with the forge. The faster I turned the crank, the hotter the fire would be. The coals would turn white with heat, as I would slow the cranking they would become a rosy red.

Jim explained, "you have to make the shoe fit the foot instead of making the foot fit the shoe. You can straighten a crooked foot some by trimming but it is natural for the horse to walk on it the way it is.

Jim had a gray horse he called Skeeter. He had gotten him from Skeeter Bill Robbins, the movie actor brother of Frank "Wild Horse" Robbins. We had old Skeeter at our place to use for awhile. I went to the corral, leading him out with just a bridle on. Being in a hurry, I jumped on him bare-back, thinking I'd quickly ride out north of the place to wrangle our horses who were grazing there. In my haste, I dug my heels into his ribs, much to his disliking and he neatly unloaded me. He only made about three jumps and I was off. Time seemed to be a little more plentiful after that fracas, so I saddled him, riding off without the heels in his ribs and had no more trouble with Skeeter.

Jim Ramsay lived out his life on the ranch on Trout Creek. He continued to be active, even running wild horses when he was in his seventies. He and Bill Logan have both gone to Cowboy Heaven where they ride good horses and tend a herd of fine cattle. They probably cross trails occasionally with my Dad, Frank Robbins, Stutter'n Dick, Bill Lewis, my brothers, Short, and Chuck, Tom Pully; hey this list could go on and on.

Author on Star—Logan's horse. Logan's Ranch 1940.

I'm sure this is what they are doing, because Heaven is supposed to be complete happiness and these guys wouldn't be happy doing anything else.

Chiltons

Chilton's had ranches about 30 miles north of Rock Springs. Dad's first job was lambing out a band of ewes. He slept out in a sheep herder's teepee on Steamboat Mountain. The spring weather was cold and rainy up there. He wrote letters home telling us about everything. He said Chiltons had a boy about my age who would be there when school was out. Bill Chilton suggested that I could come out there to spend the summer. Nothing would suit me any better. I could hardly wait for school to end.

By the time I arrived at Chilton's ranch, they had moved Dad to the Hooten place near the Boar's Tusk. He was working with the cattle and horses with Spearo Martinez, who was the foreman. Speed, as he was called, was a fine Mexican man and we hit it off very good right from the start. He always packed a 38 Smith & Wesson on his right hip when he rode away from the ranch. He wore silver mounted spurs with big rowels that jingled when he walked.

The crew mounted up at the Hooten Place.
Chuck on Blue Dog, Speed on Chief, Don on Buck, Dad on Bob, Me on Speck and Calvin Chilton standing.

Calvin Chilton was a little taller than I and slim of build. He had never done much riding but had gone with his dad a lot in the pickup hauling supplies to the ranches and sheep camps. He had a little appaloosa gelding that was gentle but had never been ridden. One of our first projects was to break him. After a couple of long cattle drives he was ready for anybody to ride him.

Don came out and worked for Chiltons too, and Chuck was at a cabin in the Sand Hills a few miles away working for Dearth. We had quite a family affair around there.

I went and stayed a couple of nights with Chuck. Everything had to be taken in by team or pack horse. The place was completely surrounded by sand dunes. It was a neat little place with pole corrals, a one room log cabin and a log barn. There was quite an acreage of lush meadow nestled among the sand hills. The sand hills were almost like snow, drifting with the wind, causing the hills to shift positions and take on different shapes. In the winter the snow gets mixed up and covered with the sand. In the summer it melts slowly and makes small lakes and water holes in the low places. These make real good watering holes for livestock.

We stayed at the Hooten place for about two weeks and gathered most of the gentle bunches of horses. There were a lot of them on White Mountain and around the tables.

Later we moved up onto Steamboat Mountain. It was a hot day and the deer flies and gnats were really thick as we rode through the sand hills. Old Pappy, the horse I was riding was thirsty and waded into a water hole until he was belly deep. He then flopped down in it, with me still on. I came out of there about as wet as I could get. After the horse's thirst had been satisfied, I no longer complained of the heat; the water evaporated from my clothes and cooled me very quickly. We continued on towards the gap on the west side of the mountain. By the time we reached the foot of it, I was quite dry, a fact greatly appreciated as we climbed to the higher altitude and cooler air. We also lost the deer flies and gnats somewhere along the way.

The ranch on Steamboat was only used in the summer time. The snow gets too deep in the winter, making it impracti-

The Johnson homestead cabin.

cal for anyone to live there. There was a good set of corrals and a one room log cabin with dirt floor, which housed the kitchen and the cook. There was another log building, used as a bunk house. This is where we slept. This was a "bring your own mattress" type of a place. I think we mostly used hay on the bunks to pad the hips and backs from the rough wood bottoms of the bunks. Located about a hundred yards north of the cabin was a spring of very cold water. Drinking water was carried from the spring to the cabin. The spring was also used for keeping perishables such as butter, milk and occasionally a water melon. These perishables were put into buckets and hung in the water of the spring. Iced tea was delicious, using the ice cold water to prepare it.

Our first project on Steamboat was rounding up cattle and branding the calves. Calvin Chilton and I rode together looking for cattle and bringing them to the ranch. We enjoyed riding together. The very first ride took us to the Johnson Canyon. The old log house of the Johnson's homestead was still pretty much intact. Nobody had lived there for years and it would take a lot of work to make it habitable. I often visualize the departed homesteaders turning over in their graves if they had seen the condition of the places they worked so hard to build up.

After the cattle roundup we started rounding up horses. They had several bunches of gentle horses which we gathered and branded the colts with Chiltons brand. Many of the horses were on White Mountain. We tried to bring them off the mountain at Chicken Springs where it wasn't too steep. We would take them past the Boar's Tusk and corral them at the Hooten place. They didn't always cooperate. We had many a wild ride off the mountain where it is pretty steep. Many of them ranged around the tables and Pine Canyon.

After the gentle bunches were done, we went down into the Red Desert and tried a few wild bunches of mustangs. They were hard to bring that far west. It was off their range and they fought real hard to get back. Usually they won. We did corral a few but finally gave it up. I'm sure that is when Dad decided to build a corral on the dessert.

The Pet Antelope

Dad had been at Chilton's Ranch for about three weeks before he asked Bill for a few days off. He wanted to go home to check on the family. He wanted to know everything was running smoothly in his absence. Bill said he would need a few days to get a man to relieve him. The ewes in the herd were mostly all done lambing and didn't require a lot of attention, but they surely needed to be herded and guarded from coyotes. The coyotes liked to kill the young lambs and feast on them.

During the time it took for Bill to find a replacement for Dad at the sheep herder's teepee, the weather turned bad. Bad for the baby lambs, calves and also for the wild life, which also had their young in the early spring.

While riding around the herd one chilly blustery morning, Dad startled a doe prong horn antelope which had given birth to a pair of fawns. The mother quickly ran over a ridge with one fawn in hot pursuit, but the other little fellow, which was much smaller and weaker, couldn't keep up.

Dad viewed the situation from a distance, wondering if the doe would come back to care for her other twin. He felt bad about spooking her, but he wished she would return and show concern for the baby. After completing his routine check of the sheep, he rode back to where he had last seen the fawn. He had hopes that she would be back, but no such luck. She was nowhere to be seen. The fawn was walking in circles bleating for it's mother.

The thought of the cold rain, which was falling with a slight mixture of snow being pushed by a stiff breeze, dampening the frail little creature, as well as the danger of coyotes in the area, persuaded Dad to take it to the teepee where it could be warm and dry.

Examining it as he would a newborn lamb which appeared weak, he discovered the fawn's little black tongue was cold. His stomach was gaunt, which led Dad to believe the doe had

34

never mothered and
nurtured him. Canned
milk, warmed and fed
with a spoon was the
best Dad had to offer.
The little fawn thrived
on it and was soon fol-
lowing him around like
a puppy dog.

When he came
home for his short visit
with us, he brought the
antelope fawn for us to
enjoy as a pet. He had
picked up a bottle and
nipple on his way
through Rock Springs.
The little buck liked
fresh cow's milk fed
from the bottle.

The pet antelope.

He was soon pick-
ing at the green spears of grass which were being coaxed up by
the warm rays of the sun.

We began calling him Buck. When feeding time came, we
would call, "Here, Buck" and he would come running.

The fawn grew and the alfalfa grew. This was his favorite
place to hide. The alfalfa soon became taller than he was in the
laying down position. We would call him and he would pop up,
appearing to come out of nowhere. He was always ready to eat
and then play for awhile before returning to his hiding place in
the alfalfa field. As the summer progressed, he began to get
hard buttons where the horns had begun to grow on his head.
We wondered if he would eventually get mean with his horns.
Jim and Wanda Ramsay had tamed a buck deer fawn. It was a
wonderful pet until his antlers developed into a series of hard
sharp points. He became very aggressive and mean with them
and had to be taken to a zoo. We didn't want that to happen to
our buck antelope.

The antelope enjoyed a good run, having the ability to out run everybody and most everything on the place. We had a litter of pups from Queenie. One of the hounds we used to catch coyotes. One of the pups really enjoyed playing with the antelope which also enjoyed a good chase.

One day while they were playing, they came to a fence while running at full speed. The antelope went under the wire fence at the same time the nearly full grown hound pup jumped over, landing on the antelope, knocking him down. We ran quickly to where the accident had happened but the buck didn't get up. He had a broken neck. We felt very bad about that incident and many tears were shed.

We dug a grave near the bank of Trout Creek, where it wouldn't be disturbed. We made a cross with Buck's name on it and erected it at the head of his grave.

Stutterin' Dick

Dick must have been about 70 at the time I met him. He came riding into the Chilton Ranch on Steamboat Mountain, rode up alongside a big old rock and slowly dismounted upon it. He had ridden over from Clemmens Casa Grandes' Ranch at Black Rock Butte. He hadn't stayed at Black Rock very long because someone else was there and the other fellow and Clemens talked in a foreign tongue Dick called Tyroll, which he didn't understand. It didn't take very much of this to make Dick feel left out and very much out of place, so he saddled up and rode to the Steamboat Ranch with hopes of finding someone to visit with.

Dick had never been a big man and now, at his age, was quite stooped over and somewhat stiff from years in the saddle. Any practical person would think he should trade the tall

The cabin housed the cooks quarters and the kitchen.

37

brown horse for a smaller horse. To mention this was a quick way to start a war with Dick because that horse and the dog that faithfully followed his master were like family to him. He would never part with either of them.

The pack animal he led was a stocky built sorrel horse with three stocking feet and a blaze face. Upon his back was a neatly assembled pack consisting of two rawhide panniers and a big bed roll. This was all Dick had to his name except a little roan gelding that was running loose down around Black Rock Butte.

I offered to help him move his gear into the bunk house but he said "By Gawd, I'm g-g-g-going to sleep outside. With winter c-c-coming on I want to get toughened up." You didn't have to be around him long to discover why he was known as Stutterin' Dick. I admired his courage and spunk for wanting to sleep outside.

By the time Dick had arranged his bed roll and cared for his horses, Frank Montoya, the cook, had supper ready to serve. He had prepared a Dutch oven full of ham hocks and beans. The aroma of the boiling pot plus the hot sour-dough bread was very appealing to the appetite.

I'll never forget the scene as we took our places around the wooden table with it's oil cloth covering. The whole room was dimly lighted by one kerosene lamp in dire need of a good chimney cleaning. This was the era during which Oleomargarine made it's first appearance upon tables across the country. In it's original form it looked like lard, coming in a one pound carton with a capsule of yellow dye to be worked into the margarine to make it look like butter. The dye didn't seem to make it taste like butter so consequently it was seldom added. As the food was passed around each of the hands took what he wanted.

As the hot bread was passed around it was followed by the Oleo. Frankie, the cook, noticed that Dick hadn't taken any of the margarine. When asked if the margarine hadn't been passed to him, Dick said, "B-b-b Gawd I don't eat it. It's only good for greasing wagons." This got a big laugh out of the whole crew.

We had a good visit that night. As a little boy Dick had lived with his Dad on the Hooten place that now belonged to Chiltons.

The place had a good spring of water on it making it an ideal stopping place for Indians as they traveled north to the mountains in summer and back to the cedar breaks of Southern Wyoming and the natural refuge of Brown's Park in Northern Colorado to spend the winters in a milder climate.

Dick said he was always afraid when the Indians would come. His Dad was usually gone riding for cattle so Dick would go inside the dugout cabin and roll a big rock against the door. They never did bother him or anything around the place. They would be gone the next morning, usually leaving a thin tired out pony on the meadow for Dick to ride.

As a young cowboy he had spent several nights in the camp of Butch Cassidy. Butch had a camp at Black Rock and when Dick would ride that country for cattle he would stay over night with the outlaw gang. He said he had never met a nicer guy to talk to, always treated his friends right and was a man of his word. Black Rock Butte was a natural place for the outlaw gang to hole up.

Mother Nature had provided them with a spring of fresh water to drink, grass for their horses and plenty of sage chickens and antelope to eat. The most important thing was several hundred yards to the Southwest, the Black Rock Butte. This was a natural fortress, a volcanic formation rising to about 400 feet above the desert floor. There is a gradual rise of about 300 feet consisting mostly of lava rock and brush, then straight up 75 to 100 feet.

At the North side is a crack in the rocks that will let a man climb to the top. It looks flat on top and probably 200 yards across. I looked it over one day and there was a long piece of hay rope hanging down through the crack. It looked very rotten so I didn't attempt to go on top of the butte.

The outlaw gang would have no worries of a posse catching them once they had someone on top of Black Rock. A sentry would be able to see for miles in every direction and the gang could hold off a small army by just guarding the crack at the North side.

Dick said if we ever saw his little roan gelding around Black Rock, we should pick him up and use him. He would be easy to spot because there weren't many roans in that part of the country. He had three stocking legs and a blaze face and branded on the left jaw.

He said, "I c-c-c-can't sell him or even g-g-g-give him to you but you can use him as long as you want to and bring him to me when you are done with him. I call him my candy horse because he looks like peppermint candy."

At this stage of Dick's life, he was too old to be hired as a working hand, so he was on what I'll call a retirement circuit. He knew every rancher from South Pass to the Colorado border and was liked by everyone.

While the weather was nice, he would ride from ranch to ranch; sheep camps, cow roundup camps and horse camps. His stays were usually short, from a couple of days to a week. He was careful not to wear out his welcome at any one place.

The people in this area were always glad to see Dick ride in. He was usually carrying "word of mouth" news about the countryside. This was always welcome in the territory where there were no telephones, no mail delivery and few radios.

Dick didn't stay more than a couple of days at Steamboat. One morning he just rode off as unexpectedly as he had ridden in. He said he was going to ride north to Pacific Spring. There he would visit sheep herders as they returned from summer range in the mountains. They would be headed for the sand hills and Red Desert to winter.

The next winter, Dick had been visiting a couple of ranch hands at a cabin. They got into an argument and Dick rode out in a huff. It was snowing, but he would go to Steamboat Bills and spend a few days. The weather worsened and became a full-fledged Wyoming blizzard.

Dick missed Bill's place in the storm and drifted east. People searched for him after the storm, but didn't find him. The next summer, someone found his bridle tied to a big sage bush just off Bush Rim. He had gone ten or twelve miles past Bill's place.

The bodies of Dick and his faithful friend, Pup were close together. They had evidently both perished in the storm.

Old Snort, his horse, probably took up with wild horses. I have never heard any more of him. I'm sure Dick was missed by his many friends who relied upon him for a bit of news and his usual good humored personality.

Coopers

Short continued to look for a job as a ranch hand, even after old Whitey left him stranded down by the Green River. He heard that Adam Cooper was looking for somebody for general ranch work. Cooper lived east of Ramsay's, probably twenty five miles, as the crow flies. Short rode over there with a good recommendation from Jim Ramsay. He was put right to work.

The ranch where he was first assigned work was in a remote canyon near a little creek which drains south east from Quaking Aspen Mountain. This whole layout was south of Rock Springs. The main job he had was irrigating hay land.

Alfalfa grew well in the soil of the canyon as long as the water was applied liberally. The water was supplied from the creek which originated higher up the canyon and was fed by snow melt from Quaking Aspen mountain and several springs also located up the canyon from the ranch. A dam had been built in the creek above the ranch to divert water down a main ditch past the meadows which were to be watered.

Small ditches were opened up from the main ditch to irrigate the individual fields. Short's job was to channel the water to the various fields, being sure the water was distributed evenly to all of the crops. A small portion was done each day until the acres had all been watered. Then he would start over again. Short would ride a horse up to the fields, wearing rubber boots and carrying a long handled sand shovel over his shoulder. This work was done at the crack of dawn and at dusk. The water was allowed to run all night. He always hoped it wouldn't break out where it wasn't needed, or digging a ditch where it wasn't wanted.

Most of the time during the day he didn't have a job to do. He was breaking a couple of horses for Cooper, as well as one for himself. Jim Ramsay had given him a five year old black mustang stallion he had caught in the Marsh country, west of Little Mountain. They had gelded him and halter broke him

42

while Short was still at Ramsay's. He had taken him along to Cooper's ranch hoping to get enough time to finish breaking him there.

The job at Cooper's ranch was not necessarily hard work, but it was lonesome for Short, who being from a large family and still a very young man was used to having people around. He was also breaking the horses and being alone was not good. He asked his boss if it would be all right to bring me out to stay with him after the school term was out. Cooper agreed to this, probably realizing how lonesome it could be.

Ike Brooks picked me up at our house in Blairtown, a coal mining suburb of Rock Springs. The trip to the Brooks home ranch was a long rough ride in the pickup truck.

Adam Cooper and Ike Brooks ranched together but they each had land and livestock individually as well. Short had ridden down to the Brooks place, bringing a saddle horse for me to ride back. We had supper at the Brooks Ranch. The ranchers were both bachelors but Adam had prepared a meal fit for a King. We spent the night at the home ranch leaving early the next morning for the ranch where Short was doing the irrigating. The cool, brisk morning air gave me an accelerated feeling as we took off on a fast trot.

It had been several months since I had been on a horse and I was very happy to be where I was that morning. The ranch in the canyon where Short was staying, was about ten miles away with quite a gain of altitude. The air felt cooler as we rode toward the mountain.

We arrived at the ranch to discover the beaver had dug a trench through one of the ditches, allowing the water to flow back into the creek, instead of being allowed to water the hay crop. They had a plan for the water which evidently would satisfy their needs by putting more water in the beaver dams which were located a little farther down stream. It was easy to tell the beaver had done the damage to the ditches by the foot prints and where their paddle shaped tail dragged in the mud. The remainder of the fore noon was spent repairing the ditch.

After dinner we decided to work with Short's bronc. We would snub him up to the saddle horn of another horse and

Chuck with L to R: Short's Black, Old Appy and Chilton mare.

Short would ride him. This method of starting a horse is used quite often, and usually successfully. The black was a pretty horse, weighing about a thousand pounds and built just the way you like them for a saddle horse. He had pin ears and a wild look about his eyes; which indicated we might have a struggle with him if he chose to be uncooperative. The saddle went on easy. Short had worked with him enough to have most of the spook out of him. I was on the snubbing horse with several wraps of the halter rope around the saddle horn. The black was snubbed up really close and seemed to be uncomfortable. Short stepped up on him and we moved out a few steps. That is when I decided to give him a little slack. He was very quick to take advantage of the slack and started to buck and jump. He couldn't get his head down to really buck, but he jumped around in a swinging motion which had a whip cracking effect throwing Short off over his tail. This was when I learned that I didn't understand all I knew about snubbing up a horse.

Short rode him after that. He'd pull leather to stay on, but the horse never gave up. When Short went to the army in World War II, he turned him out. The old Black probably went back to the Marshes and died of old age.

Jacob William Price

Dad, as he was known to all of us kids, was born, October 30, 1894 on a farm near Hitchcock, South Dakota, to William and Edith Price. He had an older half brother, Guy Olin, who was Grandma's son by a previous marriage. Uncle Guy was a carpenter by trade, making his home in Walnut Grove, Minn. He was a confirmed bachelor, seemed a bit eccentric to me. What kind of man wouldn't become interested enough in some local belle to kindle a flame in her heart, which would be certain to lead to matrimony? One of the many things we have learned to appreciate is, that all men were not created alike. Uncle Guy was happy to be a bachelor.

Dad's sister, Flossie, married Sam Ball. Their children were, Melvin, Alta and Willard. The children were very young, with Willard being just a baby, when Flossie and Sam died of the flu, during the epidemic. Melvin and Alta were taken by Grandpa and Grandma Price to raise. They figured Willard would adapt easier in someone else's home, since they felt they couldn't raise all three of them.

A family named Amacher raised Willard with their own children. Dad's sister, Hazel, married Adolph Reimath, a big man who was known to all as Tiny. To this union a son was born, and given the name Marvin. He also was a little oversized and has been called Moose by his family and friends from high school days. Dad lost a sister in infancy. Her name was Alice.

Dad entered school at age seven, at a time when age wasn't much of a factor. Some kids started at eight or nine, or whenever they found the time and the desire at the same time, consequently, there were boys several years older than Dad in the class. This proved to be very interesting because some of the students were bigger than the teacher and much stronger.

He told of one boy who had trouble with spelling. The only way he could get the lesson was to memorize it from beginning to end. The teacher knew he was doing this and asked the boy

45

to spell orally in front of the class. All went well, until the teacher changed positions of some of the words. The teacher called hammer, the boy spelled pound, the teacher called pound and the boy spelled hammer. The whole school burst out laughing. It was no doubt funny to everyone except the poor guy who was having the trouble learning.

Dad told of one man teacher they had, who tried to rule with an iron hand. The boys would go ice skating on the creek during noon hour, occasionally arriving a few minutes late for the bell. The teacher finally banned their skating during the noon break, forbidding them to leave the school grounds. The teacher was a smoker who tried to hide the fact from the kids by smoking inside the old two holer, which sat out behind the school house. The kids all knew what took so long in the toilet. One crispy, cold day the boys decided to go to the creek to skate. Gathering up their skates, they waited just long enough for the teacher to make his daily pilgrimage to the little house. Four of these big boys hit the old two holer from behind, tipping it over on the door with the half moon cut in it, trapping the flabbergasted teacher inside. they continued to the creek, looking back occasionally to see the teacher shaking his fists, first out one hole, then the other. He was calling out threats, but they weren't too concerned. After they had their game, they sat the old biffy up to it's original position. The school teacher was given ample time for his temper to cool, as he watched the hockey game from his cramped position. It was school as usual the rest of the day, after everyone had taken their seats. He wasn't nearly as strict after that incident which proved to him, they weren't afraid of him.

Dad didn't put in a lot of years in school, probably finishing the eighth grade before striking out on his own to fulfill his dream of becoming a cowboy.

Dad used to tell us kids of these strange happenings on cold winter nights as we sat in the dimly lighted tent at the horse camp. The kerosene lamp didn't put out a very bright light. The stove would be crackling, with a slight roar to it as the draft drew the smoke up the chimney. The warmth along with the almost musical sound would make us relaxed and drowsy and we would turn in early.

I recall one cold stormy night. We had finished our chores of feeding horses, dogs and cutting plenty of heavy sagebrush for wood to burn in the stove. The wind was blowing out of a dark and threatening sky from the northwest. We had no more than gotten our warm coats off when the snow began to hit the side of the tent. We were cozy inside with a crackling fire burning in the stove. Dad put the old cast iron skillet on the hot stove, placing the lid on the pan, while reaching into the make-shift cupboard for the popcorn with the other hand.

We didn't have popcorn in camp very often, and Dad seemed to know when to make a special occasion out of it. This would be a long night starting early with the stormy sky. We figured the storm could last all night and probably all of the next day. The kernels began to pop and Dad began moving the skillet back and forth across the stove lids in quick motion to keep the kernels from sticking to the bottom of the pan. If they would stick, they would soon be burned.

The corn popped slowly at first, then gradually increased to a frenzy, while Dad vigorously shook the pan. Just as quickly as it had started to pop, it slowed to just a few pops per second. I got the big bowl from the cupboard and Dad poured the fluffy white kernels into it. Next, he quickly melted butter in the already hot skillet and poured it over the corn. a little salt set it off to perfection. We ate out of the big bowl while the storm raged on, proving that it was a strong threatening force to be feared and respected by all living creatures on the Desert.

We ate quietly until the corn was about gone, then Dad began telling of an experience he had when he was a young man living in South Dakota. Growing up on a farm he always had horses and loved a fast horse and enjoyed a good horse race. He had a little cow pony, one that could turn on a dime and leave you a nickel change.

A caravan of gypsies was camped near where Dad lived. They also like fast horses and had big strong teams pulling their wagons. The gypsies were traders of almost everything. Most people were leery of them, believing them to be thieves.

Dad said this was because of their wandering nature. They were "here today and gone tomorrow" type of people, but he believed most of them to be honest.

One day Dad and a couple of his friends were racing their horses on a dirt road, not far from the gypsy camp. Two of the gypsy boys came riding over where the racing was taking place. They were mounted on a couple of long legged, high spirited thoroughbred horses.

After observing for awhile, they approached Dad and his friends to ask if they might enter the race. The said they would bet $10.00 on their horses. Dad and his friends said they didn't have the money to put up, all of them being horseman enough to know they wouldn't have a chance to win against the thoroughbreds. The one gypsy was persistent and wanted to race. He kept eyeing Dad's little horse, which he obviously had taken a liking to. He said "If you don't have money, I'll bet my saddle against yours." Finally Dad said "I'll race you. I'll bet my horse against yours. We'll race to the corner and back. The finish line will be right here." They drew a line across the road where the finish line was to be. The other gypsy and Dad's other friend rode to the corner about 1/4 mile away to see that they both went to the proper turn around point.

Dad's friend was to start the race by announcing "1, 2, 3, GO!" The thoroughbred became fired up and nervous when he realized there was going to be a race. He was hard to get lined up alongside Dad's horse, which was as calm and cool as a cucumber. They finally got off to a good even start. Dad's horse was running good, but was a good three lengths behind when they reached the turn around point. The thoroughbred was just getting warmed up good by the time he reached the corner. It took another 1/8 mile to turn him around. Upon reaching the intersection on the road, Dad brought his cow pony to an abrupt stop, wheeled him around and was patiently waiting at the finish line when the somewhat disgruntled gypsy arrived.

In those days it was the law of the land, if you bet on a horse race and lost, you had better be ready to relinquish whatever you had bet. Consequently the two gypsies rode back to camp on one horse, leaving Dad the owner of a very fine thoroughbred horse.

When the last bell rang to sound the ending of his education, he saddled up his horse, packed enough food to last a few days, tied a small bedroll behind his saddle and headed southwest to Gann Valley, SD.

Gann Valley was a hustling and bustling town at the time. It proudly incorporated two banks, a couple of hotels, general stores, livery stables, restaurants and the general businesses which make up a prairie town. Many of them built in anticipation of the coming of the railroad, wanting to be there first with the most with the arrival of the first iron horse. Their dreams were shattered when it was learned Gann Valley was destined to be an inland town. The railroad company had decided it wasn't feasible to build a road into this settlement which so eagerly awaited its arrival, believing it would be a financial boom to the whole community.

After stabling his horse at the first livery he came to, Dad made his way to the nearest hotel, determined to have a bath, a hot meal and a good night's rest in a good bed.

He was up early the next morning feeling somewhat apprehensive about leaving his horse in the hands of strangers in this little western town. Arriving at the stable he found the horse had been well cared for and was munching on a manger full of green and well cured hay. Dad struck up a conversation with the livery stable man as he went about his duties of feeding horses and cleaning the stalls of the horses that had been tied in them over night. These were mostly privately owned horses that had been ridden in or driven, hitched to wagons or buggies. The owners would call for them, picking up the bill for the stabling fee plus the feed they had consumed, after their business was finished in town.

The livery stable also had horses and buggies to rent out as well as draft horses and freight wagons, for anyone who needed them. These horses were turned together in a big corral with access to feed and water. At night they were pastured inside a fence, just outside of town.

Dad inquired about the availability of ranch work in the Gann Valley area. The stable hand directed him to the ranch of George Nelson. The place was located just off the east side of the trail, a few miles north of town. The place has become known as the High Way Ranch, in later years.

It was mid morning when Dad rode out of Gann Valley, headed in the direction of the Nelson spread. As he crested the last hill bringing the ranch site into view, he was surprised at the size of the barn on the place. The livery man had told him it had a big barn, but this was huge.

As he rode into the yard, he could see activity in the corrals and rode directly to the corral where the hands were roping and branding colts. As Dad drew nearer the activity, he could see a system being worked out by the three men in the corral.

One cowboy was front footing the colts, catching both front feet in the loop of his lariat, pulling it tight and throwing the young horse to the ground. Another man was on the colt's head instantly holding it down while the roper tied both front feet and one hind foot tightly together with his lariat. This colt was going nowhere until it had been branded. One man's job was tending the fire and tending the branding irons. The fire was started early, allowing the wood to burn down to a bed of brilliant red coals. The irons had to be watched closely so they didn't get too hot. An overheated iron applied to a young animal's hide can make a sore, causing the brand to blot because of surplus scarring of the area. A brand which uses an enclosure, such as an A or O will blot very easily. If the brand is small it will blot easier than a large brand. A brand properly applied, burns through the hair, burning the hide just enough to cause it to scab over and peal off. The hair soon grows in, but thinner than it had been before the branding took place. The animal carries this brand for the rest of it's life. This was the only way early day ranchers had of identifying their stock on the open range.

Dad watched the branding, not wanting to interrupt the on going operation. When they had finished the colt they were branding and it had been turned loose to return to it's mother,

George Nelson walked over to ask Dad what he wanted. Dad expressed his desire to work and was put right to work.

George said he had homesteaded there and when rumors of a railroad made it sound like it would really happen, he too jumped at what he considered an opportunity to flourish. He had built the huge barn, sunk a well which supplied water to a tank on the hill above the ranch. He had planned to go into the dairy business and ship his milk by rail. After the railroad failed to build, he utilized the facilities for general ranch use. The barn was good protection for livestock in the harsh South Dakota winters. The water system supplied ample water for the livestock and the people who worked to produce it.

The life of a cowboy wasn't as romantic and glorious as Dad had always believed it to be. The school bell hadn't really brought an end to his education. It had only helped him into a new phase of his education. Fence building and stacking hay were just as much work on the ranch as it had been back home on the farm. He toughed it out though, with the realization that there would be riding and roping in the fall, when the cattle and horses would be rounded up for branding, doctoring and marketing.

There was very little land under fence in that part of the country in the early 1900's. The cattle and horses were free to roam in any direction. One of their favorites was to range south and west into the Missouri River breaks. The grass was good there, with ample water supply. The breaks provided good shelter from adverse weather conditions which frequent the area.

Dad had always liked horses, riding the horses on his Dad's farm at home. He "cowboyed" them every chance he got, making them buck by spurring them. He often got into trouble with Grandpa Price for this. All in all, he was a prime candidate for a job on a real working ranch. The one who broke the horses to saddle was of special interest to him. They didn't rough them out, instead they tried to keep them from bucking while they were breaking them.

The bronc twister, as he was called, told Dad, "If you think you need to practice riding broncs, pick a spoiled old saddle horse that knows nothing but bucking, and is no good to use. If you spur a good horse, chances are he will be practicing too, and he might get better at bucking than you are at riding. Then we will have another spoiled horse on our hands.

Dad put in two years in the Gann Valley area, breaking horses and riding rough string for a couple of outfits. He met Bill Maher at a rodeo in Ft. Pierre and they started riding in as many rodeos as they could find. They finally decided to put together a rodeo of their own, each contributing his share of the bucking stock and the working stock, such as pick up horses. They split partnership after a few years but remained friends. In later years they teamed up to produce several rodeos.

Dad married Bertha Glaze in 1914. Neither of them probably ever dreamed they would become the parents of eight kids. They accepted each of us as we arrived, nurturing us with loving care and understanding. A swift kick in the rear for improper behavior, or a slap on sassy lips were also instrumental in guiding us to adulthood. Neither did us any harm because we didn't get it if we didn't have it coming.

In the early thirties drought had hit the western and central area of South Dakota really bad. The eastern section wasn't hit as bad. They were able to grow feed in that area so Dad bought a truck and hauled grain and hay to the drought area. The money situation was bad and kept getting worse, leaving him unable to collect for the loads he was hauling. About this time, he ran across Ben Brunie of Sioux Falls, South Dakota. Ben was a rodeo producer who needed someone to truck bucking stock for him. Dad took the job but things just got worse. Dad couldn't make the payments and lost his truck. As I think back about the hard times we went through, I'm reminded of a Christmas while I was quite young. In fact, I hadn't started school yet. We were living on the place near the river. Dad was working on some kind of project in the back room. My curiosity got the best of me, so I went in to see what he was doing. He continued to work until I asked what he was building. He said it was a beaver trap. I thought to myself, a strange looking beaver trap, but if Dad said it is a beaver trap, that's what it is. He gave it a couple of coats of paint. I couldn't imagine why a beaver trap would have to be painted.

Jake Price

When Christmas morning arrived I discovered that Santa had come and had left two beautiful dolls for my sisters. Apparently he couldn't find a crib to put them in so he had put them in Dad's beaver trap. Mamma had sewn a mattress and blankets just to fit. We all had a good laugh about the beaver trap being Dad's way of protecting his secret from the girls. He no doubt thought I would tell them if I knew what he was building. That year I got a toy, wind up crawler tractor, with rubber tracks. It was a small, hand held toy that I really enjoyed.

Christmas was always an enjoyable time for us kids growing up. We didn't realize times were hard, because everyone was in the same boat. We didn't have indoor plumbing, but even then there was recycling. It's surprising how quickly last years mail order catalog became toilet paper. Even better yet were the little soft tissues that came wrapped around the peaches in the crate.

Many of our Christmas gifts were hand made. The longer I live, the more I have learned to appreciate the home made gifts. Dad enjoyed fishing and hunting, besides it brought in a little income. One time when the hounds had chased a big dog coyote for most of a cold wintry morning, the old coyote decided he had been pushed a little too hard and took refuge inside a steel culvert which passed under a roadway. The hounds were all too big to enter the culvert. This brought on much frustration and excitement for the hounds as they went back and forth across the road, smelling in one end of the culvert, then the other. Dad decided to devise a way to bring the coyote out into the open. Going to a nearby fence, he cut off about thirty feet of barbed wire. He began pushing the wire into one end of the culvert with a twisting motion. When the wire finally made contact with the coyote, it became entangled in his fur. this was Dad's plan and it was working beautifully except that by the time he had extracted Mr. Coyote from the culvert, the hounds being tired anyway, had lost interest in the whole escapade and had gone to lie in the tall grass. This left just Dad and the coyote. As the coyote came out, securely held by the wire tightly wound into his fur, he was fighting mad. Dad had

Chuck with hat on and Don with furs, guns and hounds. Note: coyote and badger furs.

no weapon near enough to reach, as he had been depending on the hounds to be there to grab Mr. Coyote when he emerged from the culvert. Instinctively he grabbed for the animal's throat. Instinctively the coyote grabbed for Dad's gloved hand, sinking sharp teeth clear through glove and hand. Dad hung on with his left arm around the coyote's neck. The coyote held Dad's hand clamped firmly in his powerful jaws. This is the way it was when Chuck came riding up on a tired saddle horse. He had been following the hounds, but had stopped to let his horse rest when Dad had taken over the chase. After prying the coyote's jaws open to free Dad's hand, they killed the coyote, loaded the hounds into the back of the truck and went home.

Mother tried to get Dad to go to Hitchcock to Doc Scheib, but Dad said he would be all right. They washed it with creosote dip, a disinfectant used mainly on livestock. Dad didn't have much to do with doctors, preachers, or politicians. The hand healed slowly with bits of yellow fragments of cloth from his glove, working their way out of the wound.

Chuck and Don had skinned the coyote and put it on a stretcher while Dad's wound was being cleaned and dressed. Animals skin much easier when they are still warm, than if they are allowed to get cold or worse yet, to be allowed to freeze. Coyotes are skinned differently than badgers. Badgers are split down the belly and legs, leaving it wide open to be tacked up on the side of a building or a wide, flat board to dry. The coyote skin is supposed to look like he just crawled out of it. It is then put on a stretcher, which somewhat resembles an ironing board. It is usually made of two boards hinged in the middle with an adjustable brace across the wide end. This enables the fur to be stretched after it is pulled onto the stretcher. Care was used in skinning and handling the furs to protect them from cutting or tearing, or making more holes in the skin than were absolutely necessary. Extra holes cut down the value considerably.

Dad always took pride in marketing furs which were free of knife cuts and also clean of flesh and fat, which also detract from the quality of the hides.

As I Remember Mamma

Benoni "Ben" and Cordelia Glaze were my mother's parents. The family consisted of two sons named William and Milton and the daughter, Bertha who was our mother.

Milton was unmarried and worked at the local pool hall in Hitchcock, South Dakota. He died at an early age. Grandma always said it was his smoking and the smoke from the pool hall that ruined his health.

William, better known as Bill, was married to Addie Sweeten. They had an only son named Kenneth. They also lived in Hitchcock where Uncle Bill worked in Dick Hobart's Drug Store until Hobart moved out of town. Bill would have liked to have his own drug store but found this to be not feasible because he wasn't a licensed pharmacist. He did start a store which he called, Bill's Variety Store that he operated in Hitchcock until his death.

When we were little kids in town on Saturday nights, we would always make a special trip to his store for a special treat "on the house." He was a great one to kid us and tease just a little bit.

Kenneth excelled in sports so it was natural for him to become a sports announcer for Radio Station KWAT in Watertown, S.D.

Grandpa Glaze was a farmer in the Lake Byron area until moving to Hitchock where he ran the dray. He had a team of horses for hauling freight to and from the railroad depot. He also hauled coal from the railroad coal sheds. He would haul it to homes and other places where it was burned for fuel.

Grandpa died before I was born, Kenneth is gone also, leaving no one to carry on the Glaze name.

My mother, or Mamma, as we called her, was a small woman with straight black hair, worn in bangs most of the time.

Normally she was good natured and didn't even complain when we and Dad would have corn cob fights in the house. The cobs went good when thrown, and didn't hurt much when you got hit, but it did make a heck of a mess in the house which we would all pitch in and help to clean up when the war was over.

Short was the family tease, just loving to tease our sisters just to hear them yell. One day he was teasing one of them constantly for quite some time, finally getting on Mamma's nerves. She told him to stop teasing but he kept right on with his little game. She was working at cooking something in the kitchen but could easily hear all the fuss in the next room. She said "If I come in there you will be sorry" but this didn't even slow him down. Being able to take no more of the nonsense she started in there, still carrying the long butcher knife she was using in the kitchen. When Short saw her coming, he ran and she threw the knife. It hit the wall broadside about two feet from where he had vanished out the open door. I'm sure she had no intentions of hitting him, but it sure ended the teasing for that day.

She was also good at handling horses, having been raised on a farm near Hitchcock, S.D. where she helped work the fields with horses. She told about sewing grain by hand. She would stand in the wagon which contained the seed and while her father drove the team, her job was to throw the seeds trying to distribute them as consistently and evenly as possible.

She said it was a boring job, and being a teen aged girl her mind would get completely off the seeding process. Her Dad would glance back occasionally to check on the kind of job she was doing. When he would catch her day dreaming, he would loudly say "throw throw" and she would throw very fast for awhile, causing the grain to be very thick in some areas and probably very thin to bare in the areas where she was day dreaming.

Several times, after we moved to Wyoming, she rode to Logans when we were in school. She would visit Lila Logan and when school was out we would all ride home together.

In the early years of my parent's marriage, she tells of driving to Hitchcock with horse and buggy. They lived on Grandpa Price's farm, located 4 1/2 miles southeast of Hitchcock, S.D. She took turns driving with a neighbor lady who lived another 2 miles farther down the road. Mamma would always walk and trot the horse so it wouldn't get sweaty and tired. The other lady would run her horse all the way to town, he would be puffing and sweaty. Mamma asked the other lady if she didn't think it was hard on the poor horse to run him all the way. Her reply was "The sooner we get there the longer he will have to rest."

Back in the days when radio was just coming into it's own, we spent a lot of time telling stories, playing games and just anything for entertainment during the day. The radio was saved for night because the reception was better at night. Another good reason for this was, we had to use the battery of the Model T Ford to run the radio.

One chilly week-end day all eight of us kids were home, most of us were inside the house, but the three older boys were outside. We had a neighbor by the name of Iver Jacobsen. Another neighbor whose name I can't recall, used to call him Jacob Iverson which was quite amusing to us. We were just discussing this and clowning around when there came a knock on the door. No one had driven in and the dogs hadn't barked so believing it to be one of the boys, Mother called out, "Come in Jacob Iverson." The door slowly opened but it wasn't one of the boys and it sure wasn't Jacob Iverson. It was another neighbor standing there looking as if he had come to the wrong place. I could see the embarrassment spread over Mamma's face as she quickly explained the situation to him. He also had a good laugh right along with the rest of us. He had walked in unnoticed by the dogs or any of us.

Mamma worked hard raising the eight of us kids, doctoring with mostly home remedies but always there when we needed her and she could always ease the pain by using her sympathetic and caring ways.

The Great Majestic was probably the most important piece of household equipment she ever had. This huge kitchen range was fired up first thing in the morning and would still be hot at bedtime, this of course after many fillings of wood, cobs or coal. The Majestic had a strong oven door that could be sat upon. You had better know, that was a popular spot on chilly mornings. All this comfort along with the aroma of freshly brewed coffee and pancakes on the griddle, makes one wonder why anyone ever left home. I've heard Mamma say many times "I bake nine loaves of bread every other day." I'm sure she was glad when the girls were old enough to help.

There were eight of us kids and it probably seemed like we picked eight different directions to go each day into this big country. She put in many a night dreaming of some of us being lost in this vast area of wilderness. We were instructed to always carry matches. If we got lost or injured or for any reason we couldn't make it home, we were supposed to light a fire which would be easily seen by anyone searching for us. This was a good idea but fortunately good luck prevailed and none of us became helplessly lost or any such catastrophes.

As I think back on what a seemingly frail person she was, I can't help but think, what a solid rock she was in the foundation of our family. We were so fortunate to have such a loving set of parents. They weren't great on saying "I love you" or outwardly showing affection but we knew we were loved, actions speak just as plainly as words. They were always quick to praise us for a job well done.

It had to be heart breaking to Mamma when we left her elderly and ailing mother to move to Wyoming, but we kids didn't sense a thing. She was strong and kept her feelings hidden very well.

Grandma Glaze, the former Cordelia Murphy, had come to Dakota Territory in a covered wagon in the 1860's. She had been born in a log cabin on the banks of the Wabash River. She told about the beautiful river and timbered countryside and how different it was from Dakota.

She had lost her mother when she was eight years old, which is about the same time they moved to Dakota Territory.

She told about one of her Dad's horses that got frightened when they crossed the Mississippi River on a ferry. Her dad had to hold it by the halter and comfort it until they reached the shore. When we got word of her death, Mamma couldn't attend Grandma's funeral in South Dakota. Within a year after Grandma's death we lost our mother. This had to be a burden on Dad who was working about 35 miles from Rock Springs,

L to R back: Harland "Short," Mother Bertha, Marcella and Charles. Front: Rozella, Jean and Elwood "Sweed."

on Chilton's ranch, but Don, Marcie and Rosie took over the household and we got along quite well.

There was a couple, by the name of Sparks, who ranched near Pinedale who wanted to adopt Sweed and Rosie. They had everything needed to provide a good home for them, but I'll always remember what Dad told them. He said "I'm going to keep them all together, these kids have just lost their mother and they aren't going to lose each other." He was grateful to the people and finally agreed to let them go to their ranch to spend a week just to see if they would like it, but there would be no adoption. As I remember, the kids came home feeling somewhat bored, and a bit home-sick. The people were good sincere folks with good intentions, but I'll have to say I always admired Dad for his stand on this very important family issue.

While Dad was working for Chiltons the second summer they invited me to tour Yellowstone Park with them. This sounded like it would be much fun, I could hardly wait to get started.

Baldy Baker

Clarence "Baldy" Baker had been a long time employee of the Chilton Ranch. He was an excellent sheep herder and all around ranch hand. He was a very likable man with a sense of humor that just wouldn't quit. Baldy too had been invited to tour Yellowstone Park with the Chilton Family.

Bill Chilton, Baldy, Calvin and I slept in one tent while the other tent was quarters for Mrs. Chilton, Marion, Ruth and Ethel.

The first night out was spent at Boulder, Wyoming where we swam in the warm pool at the hot mineral springs. We stayed in cabins located near the pool. The warm pool was fun to swim in and very relaxing. The next day we went up to check on a band of sheep Chilton's had grazing in National Forest land, near Freemont Lake. The mountains were beautiful in this area with the tall straight pine trees. This was a mature forest, with most of the trees having spent a century or more competing with the surrounding trees for sun light. This caused them to grow unusually tall and straight, appearing to challenge any intruders who might penetrate the boundaries of their domain. The sheep were doing well with the herder, Rich Vigil reporting no problem. We dropped the supplies for him at the herder's tee pee, which we had brought from Rock Springs. We set up our camp near by on the shore of beautiful Fremont Lake and proceeded to enjoy the evening. Baldy built a bon fire on the sandy beach just as the sun was sinking behind the rugged horizon. We could feel the air turn chilly as the sun went down. The chill came on fast at this high altitude and the heat from the crackling fire, kindled with dry pine wood, felt good.

Baker had herded sheep in the mountains many times and would probably have a band here now if it wasn't for the Yellowstone trip. Baldy and Rich began swapping tales about herding sheep in the mountains. I was all ears and remained

Chuck (standing) and Dad breaking a horse on Chilton's Ranch.

quiet, hoping to learn all I could about the mountains. The biggest worry of the herders was the bears that occasionally get hungry and decide to kill sheep for food. The herder's dogs can bark and stir up quite a fuss, but they are no match for a bear who can lay them wide open with one swipe of his paw, equipped with razor sharp claws. Thunder and lightning with hard rain and hail, are bad to scatter the flock, making them very hard to round up in rough country and heavy timber. There was always the threat of coyotes, mountain lions and bears, leading me to believe that herding sheep in the mountains was no picnic.

The next morning, after a camp fire breakfast we continued on, passing through Jackson which hadn't yet become a bustling tourist town. We traveled on, with the beautiful snow capped Teton Mountain to the west of us. At the South entrance gate to Yellowstone Park, Bill paid the entrance fee for everyone in the party. The park ranger asked if we had any fire arms. Bill had two rifles which were always carried in the pick-up to shoot any predator which might be a threat to the rancher's sheep.

The ranger fixed seals on the firing mechanisms, disarming them for the duration of our visit in the National Park.

The first attraction we came to in the park was the paint pots. These hot bubbly puddles of different colored clay surely deserves the name Paint Pots. Nearby were pools of clear boiling water. These all smelled strongly of sulfur, an odor that almost made you look around, "wondering who did it."

Our first night in Yellowstone Park was spent at The Fishing Bridge, named so for it's popularity as a fishing spot for tourists year after year. We had seen many bears along the road, looking for a handout. Signs everywhere said "Do Not Feed the Bears," but everywhere we went people were feeding the bears.

At the amphitheater one evening we were treated to an informative lecture on the park. The ranger said the bears were not the problem, the people were. The bears seemed so docile and friendly that people can't believe they are dangerous. They feed them bread, hot dogs or whatever they have until it is gone, but the bear is still hungry and decides to eat the fingers or hand and the person can't get away from it. Many bears had to be disposed of because of attacks on humans, so it is best not to feed them at all.

The next night was spent at the camp ground near Old Faithful Geyser. A camp fire always felt good at night, plus the aroma coming from the rapidly burning pine wood was, and still is, savored by me today.

As we sat huddled around the camp fire, toasting marshmallows, Bill and Baldy started talking about the wild horses in the Red Desert. When Bill Chilton's parents homesteaded on Steamboat Mountain, they brought along four or five good draft brood mares to be used as foundation stock. They would raise their own work horses. They also had a big stallion which would assure them of fine quality draft horses.

There was however, a drawback which would give them plenty of trouble in their plans for the future. The land was almost all open range with very little under fence, which left them vulnerable to the wild stallions from herds that roamed the area, always looking for mares to add to their harems.

The Chilton horses ranged quite close to the homestead most of the time, watering at the spring, allowing them to be seen almost every day. One morning the only one to come to the spring was the big draft horse. He was limping along slowly and obviously had been hurt. As he came closer the homesteader took a good look. He had been kicked, bitten and in general, pretty badly beaten up. His brisket was swollen from being constantly kicked. The swelling hung down like a sack full of jelly.

Mr. Chilton was furious as he and Bill saddled up two horses to begin the search for his prize mares. As he slid the 30-30 into it's scabbard, he vowed to kill the mustang that had run his mares off and beaten his stallion to a pulp.

Back tracking the stud they found a place where he had rolled, probably when he was ringing wet with sweat after the fight with the wild stallion. The tracks led to the flat west of the ranch, where the mares had been seen grazing a couple of days earlier. They rode in a huge circle, looking for tracks. The draft horses would leave a much bigger hoof print than the mustangs, making it easier to determine which way the shanghaied mares were taken. Finally they found where the battle of the stallions had taken place. Now came the hard part. Which way did they go? The riders split up, each playing his hunch and circling the battleground trying to determine which way they had gone.

Bill finally got on the hot trail, which led to the north and east. The older Chilton had ridden south and was out of earshot so Bill waited until he looked back, then waved for him to follow. The trail led to a spring on Jack Morrow Creek, about a mile below the homestead. The horses had apparently drank, then proceeded on up the east side and out of the canyon.

Bill and his Dad pushed on, wanting to find the horses before sundown. The tracks led towards the Bush Rim where the horses were spotted, grazing peacefully on the south slope of the rim. By traveling down a small wash, they were able to get quite close to the horses, where they had a good look at the stud that had caused so much trouble. The wild stallion was small compared to the brood mares, bay with a blaze face, really a pretty little horse. The older Chilton began to drag the rifle out of it's scabbard while Bill began pleading with him, not to shoot such a fine horse. I guess he had been on the trail long enough to have cooled off just a bit and agreed to spare the wild stallion's life. When the two riders appeared, the little horse took off running but the mares didn't follow him.

He couldn't figure this out so back he came and tried to herd them, biting them, with his ears laid back but they only trotted and once in awhile they broke into a gallop. Bill's Dad took the lead as he headed towards the ranch. Bill brought up the rear. The gentle mares followed the rider but the mustang stallion was all over the place. First he was with the mares, trying to get them to follow him as he ran on top of a high knoll. He snorted and whistled a couple of times then he came running back to the mares. This little horse was probably a two or three year old that had been kicked out of a herd by an older stallion. He had whipped that big stallion which had these mares and by his way of thinking they were his to keep for his own. He had earned them and wouldn't give them up easily.

Chilton rode on towards the ranch leading the mares while Bill continued to follow, not pressuring the wild horse but allowing him to remain with the mares if he chose to. All the time he was wondering what would happen when they reached the corral. It was dusk when the older Chilton rode into the corral with the mares following closely behind. The little stallion was right in among them and was corralled before he knew what had happened. Bill said they broke the mustang which turned out to be one of their best horses. With that he put the camp fire out and we went to our bed rolls where we enjoyed some more mountain air sleeping in Yellowstone Park.

We were awakened by Baldy Baker trying to chase a big brown bear out of camp. The sun was just beginning to rise as Calvin and I ran to the flap of the tent to see the bear. He was standing upright on his hind legs, reaching upwards trying to get a hold on the grub box which hung suspended from a tree branch. Baker was yelling, "You big brown rascal, get out of here." We figured, under different circumstances, he would have used much stronger language but in the presence of ladies, he restrained himself. The bear finally gave up trying to snitch breakfast and returned to the pine forest. Mrs. Chilton soon had pancakes and bacon cooking over the open camp fire. I leaned back against a log, viewing the beauty of my surroundings. The sun was just beginning to peek over the tops of the tall pines. As I savored the aroma of the food cooking over the open fire, I figured, life just don't get any better than this.

After breakfast we rolled up our bed rolls, took the tents down and loaded everything into the pickup and car to be ready to travel. We were within walking distance of the geyser so we took one of the foot paths and walked in to the geyser. It was a thrill to watch Old Faithful erupt. She was right on time as posted on the bulletin board near by. The sun shining on the water and steam as it shoots sky-ward, makes a very beautiful display of colors. It was sure quite a sight. The thing that amazes me is how it builds up steam pressure to allow it to erupt at such evenly spaced intervals. The ranger said it goes off every 50 minutes. Many of the animals gather around the geysers to keep warm in the winter. That would be a sight to behold. As they battled for supremacy, many of the predators such as coyotes, cougar and bobcats would constantly be trying to make a meal of a crippled or old animal.

Our trip home lead past Jenny's Lake, at the foot of the beautiful Tetons. We continued on to Daniel, where we set up camp near the Green River. We spent the next day at this spot where Baldy taught Calvin and I how to catch trout. Mrs. Chilton showed us how good they were, fried on the river bank.

After we passed Farson, as we continued on our way back to Rock Springs, we saw several bunches of wild horses. Most of them were quite a distance from the highway. We stopped at a shelter cabin alongside the road, put there by the highway department for the convenience to anyone who became stranded in a winter blizzard. There was a stove inside, with enough wood to see you through quite a storm. We ate our lunch while Bill Chilton explained the purpose of these shelter cabins to us. People were supposed to leave them clean and in good shape for the next party which might need it in an emergency.

I have noticed the shelters have been gone for quite a long time. It makes me wonder if the road being graded higher allowing the wind to blow the snow off the road, or perhaps vandalism was the cause for their removal. I'm sure the storms still move furiously through that country and motorists still drive in all kinds of weather. At the time we stopped there and after Bill explained their purpose, I felt they were sure a good little insurance package for anyone caught out there, who would be otherwise unprotected from the elements. On this forty mile stretch of road through open country, there is nothing for protection.

We pulled into Rock Springs with this super vacation trip behind us, leaving me feeling like it had ended all too soon. This trip was a real treat to me. I'll be forever grateful to the Chilton family for taking me along on their family vacation. Dad stayed on at Chilton's for almost two years, trapping coyotes around the sheep in the winter and working with cattle and horses during the summer months.

In 1939, we moved to Rock Springs, with both Rozella and I in high school, the folks decided it would be wise to move the family to town. This would be more feasible than boarding us out somewhere. School at Rock Springs High was all right, but the school was much bigger than I was used to. Most of which were country schools. This was also the year Momma died, which was a great loss to the family.

Blue Dog

Bill Chilton had brought supplies to the Steamboat Ranch and as usual, a certain amount of news. The thing that interested me the most was his telling about Elza Eversol, Tom Pulley, Harold Anderson and my brother Chuck, rounding up horses on the Blue Rim. The area was strange to me, being about thirty miles west of Chilton's Ranch and near the Green River.

The horses were mostly wild over in that area but it seemed to be a haven for some branded and broke horses who wanted to roam free.

Chuck was working for the I.H. Dearth Ranches of Eden Valley at the time and had been sent with the crew to help with the roundup and to keep any of Dearth's horses to be returned to the ranch.

After the roundup, Chuck told of his experiences out there. They had a camp set up near a good spring of water. The camp consisted of a sheep camp wagon and a couple of ranch type tee pees.

One evening after supper, one of the guys decided to take a rifle and walk over the hill in hopes of killing an antelope for fresh meat for the camp. As he reached the crest of the hill, he ducked down and called to the others, "come up here to see the deer." Now, deer were almost unheard of in this treeless almost barren land, so they all went running up the slope to see something unusual. As they approached the guy with the rifle, he sat there chuckling. He said "It's gone now but it was sure a dear little rabbit." They all had a good laugh, and seeing no antelope, they returned to camp where they soon crawled into their soogans and were soon put to sleep by the lonely wail of a pair of coyotes who probably felt as if their domain had been invaded by the horse wranglers.

Chuck had returned to the ranch, bringing the Dearth horses they had corralled as well as one of Chilton's, which he left at the ranch on his way to the lonely little ranch in the sand hills which belonged to Dearth. Bill Lewis had built this neat little place in the sands. It had a set of pole corrals as well as a log cabin.

The grass grew tall and lush in the lowland between the sand hills. This land was fenced off for pasture where Dearth had a small herd of dairy heifers. He kept them here, where they were isolated from the herd bulls until they were mature enough to breed. It was Chuck's job to watch them, being sure they stayed inside the fence and to be sure no stray bulls got inside. He also had to be sure they had an adequate water supply. This little ranch was vacant much of the time, except for the mice who seemed to feel their privacy was being violated when a cow hand moved in to tend cattle or horses. The cabin had only one room containing the bare essentials of house keeping for one man. Chuck tried trapping the mice, but said he could only catch a couple each night. This seemed to be such a slow process that he began turning the kerosene lamp way down, dimming the light so the mice would come out, then he would shoot them off the table with a twenty two rifle.

Dearth had a blue roan horse, which he included in the string of saddle horses he had given Chuck to take to the Blue Rim to be used in the horse roundup. He told Chuck he would buck but was a good horse with plenty of speed and good bottom, both very necessary features in a horse to be used for running wild mustangs. He said "try him down there, if he doesn't work out for you, turn him loose, he'll run with the wild horses. Maybe if you ride him plenty, he will straighten up. He sure has the makin's of a good horse." Harold Anderson knew the horse and encouraged Chuck by telling him, "if you can stay on him the first thing in the morning, you'll have a good horse under you all day long. He won't bother you until the next time you ride him." Harold said he had ridden with the hand who broke him. He said the guy carried a quirt with a shot loaded handle and continually abused the horse by hitting him along side the head with it. If he didn't perform to the cowboy's liking, or if he tried to buck, he got the shot loaded end of the quirt along side the head. He said after you have ridden him a few times, when he begins to buck, you might try to intimidate him by throwing your arm out to the side, as if you were going to hit him, and holler, "Blue Dog you S.O.B." I'm sure it won't work the first time. You are new to him and he is going to try his damndest to buck you off. Chuck had a new form fitter saddle he had ordered from the E.C. Lee Saddlery, of Ft. Pierre, S.D. His first experience with his new saddle on a rough bronc turned out, not good. I believe those form fitters with their big swell curving up over the leg, and the high cantle behind your rear end, can give a sense of false security. Add to this the fact the new leather is very slippery made for a bad situation. He had picked himself up and very disgustedly said, "what a way to break in a new saddle."

Old Blue Dog stood there, ground tied, while Chuck bridled him and put the form fitter saddle on him. He humped up his back a little as the cinch was tightened by the pulling of the latigo strap. Many well broke saddle horses will do this. Chuck led him for about one hundred yards before stepping up on him, using all of the precautions he knew to try to keep him from bucking. He surely didn't want to get bucked off in front of a bunch of seasoned cowhands like this, besides, he had hopes of this becoming a good and useful horse he could keep in his string as long as he worked for Dearth. With his reputation for bucking, he was sure nobody else would want to exercise him every morning they rode him.

Old Blue Dog bogged his head and began bucking, swapping ends and sun fishing. He tried with all of his might to unseat his rider, but Chuck figured somebody had put glue in his saddle, enabling him to weather the storm and remain on top. When it was over, it was over for the day. Chuck reined him around a few times and they were ready to round up horses.

Blue Dog was a pretty horse and Chuck liked him. He had a nice easy gait when he traveled across country, was a good camp horse and except for his bucking, was a good all around horse. Chuck said he tried to intimidate him, like Harold had suggested but it didn't seem to help. There seemed to be no set pattern to his bucking streaks. Chuck did ride him as long as he worked for Dearth.

One time he rode him to a sheep herder's camp where he stayed over night. When he mounted Blue Dog in the morning, it was the same old routine. When the horse quit bucking, Chuck rode close to the herder's wagon to bid him farewell. The Mexican herder asked, "why didn't you get off of him?" Chuck said "get off? I was having too hard of a time staying on."

Dad worried about Chuck, being alone at the Dearth cabin and riding Blue Dog. There wasn't really a mean bone in his body. He didn't kick, bite or strike and Chuck seemed to have him mastered, as far as riding him was concerned. Chuck must have had many good feelings about being able to ride this horse and work cattle with him. When Chuck went off to war, I'm sure he did a lot of thinking and talking about Blue Dog. I suppose the horse was turned loose on the Blue Rim after Chuck left. Not many cowboys would put up with a horse as unpredictable as the one Chuck fell in love with.

The <u>L</u> Stud

Raised in Kentucky with blue grass up to his knees, his life as a Kentucky thoroughbred was a little sketchy to us who only knew him as the <u>L</u> Stud on the Red Desert in Wyoming. Chances are he didn't cooperate with the pint sized jockeys with their sharp stinging quirts.

Whatever the reason he left the race tracks and fell into the hands of wild horse runners, is unknown to me.

I'm sure the new owner knew he had a prize in this fleet footed, stocking legged, bay stallion.

The horse camp was set up near Black Rock Butte just at the west edge of the Red Desert.

The "Stud" was kept on picket or hobbled at night. He was given grain and exercised daily until he became acclimated to the 7200 foot elevation. He also had a lot to learn about sage brush, rocks and badger holes. After the break-in period he was ready for the big test of running the wild ones.

I don't really know how many runs were made on the <u>L</u> Stud but I'm sure he longed for greener pastures. There was also a longing for freedom and a part of the action that would be his if he could dominate a harem of mares. There must have been many biting, kicking, squealing and bloody battles with wild stallions before accomplishing this but he was very capable and came out victorious. I never had the thrill of riding the "flying machine" of a horse. My experiences with him came later on.

We were headquartered at Bill Lewis' (Steamboat Bill's) place in the sands in the summer of "41." Dad had made a deal with Bill, we would gather horses and brand Bill's colts and we would keep the slicks. "Slicks" are unbranded horses over 1 year old. We worked on the corral at his small ranch located in the sand hills just at the southwest end of Steamboat Mountain. Bill's place consisted of a dugout cabin, a small log building for storage of supplies, a brush roofed shed and a good set of corrals but needing some repair as posts rot fast in the sand. The water supply was from a spring that didn't run much water but had been curbed up and left a 3'x3'x4' deep hole of crystal clear, ice cold water.

The corral shaped up good, we replaced the snubbing post with another real heavy post dead center in the round corral. The round corral was where the roping and branding took place. Most places that handle many horses have a round corral.

We gathered several bunches of horses from around the tables "Rock Buttes" and close to Steamboat. These horses had all been handled some and weren't very wild.

We got a few slicks and branded a lot of colts with Bill's brand ($_{OO}^{O}$) three circles on the right front shoulder.

We decided then to work farther east and eventually get into the Red Desert where about 99% of the horses would be slicks and they were all very wild.

The L Stud watched over his harem of mares from a rocky knoll near Black Rock Butte. The warm days of spring had brought about a drastic change from the cold winter. The sage brush had greened up, bringing with it's new foliage the pungent odor of the most prominent of bushes in the area. It was foaling time for the mares. Several new colts had already been born. On this special morning the black mare, the leader of the bunch, had wandered up a shallow draw to be alone and out of sight of the rest of the horses. The stud had watched her go, restraining his urge to put her back into the herd. He knew she had to be alone to successfully give birth to the colt and to care for it until it would be strong enough to travel with the herd of mustangs.

Mares have so much mothering instinct that another mare will sometimes claim a new born foal for her own. She will fight the mother of the new born thinking it belongs to her. Often the new colt is crippled in the fracas. For this reason, Mother Nature has given the mustangs the instinct to get away by themselves while they foal.

The black mare moved around restlessly, not grazing much but looking for a place to lie down. She was up and down several times, finally the contractions began and she got serious about what she had to do.

The colt was born about mid afternoon. He lie there wet and breathing hard from the strain of being born. He nickered to his mother who was on her feet immediately and began licking him and encouraging him to stand up. He raised his head and pushed his front feet out ahead of him, pushing himself upward. His legs seemed too long and spindly and he got them tangled up and fell back down. After several tries he stood up, looking almost as if somebody had propped him up with his four long legs sprawled out.

His mamma was happy to see him standing and moved closer to him to offer him his first meal of wild mare's milk. Whenever we would catch an unusually wild mustang, one that fought a lot, Dad would say "Boy, that one was raised on wild mares milk."

The colt, as wobbly as he was, worked his way along the mother's side, nuzzling her with its nose and tongue, searching for the right place to find a teat. Finally he came to the soft, warm, almost hairless flank where his searching paid off. Under the flank were two soft, but full nipples for him to feed on.

After taking on a good fill, he plopped down to rest and to completely dry off before the sun slipped down behind Spring Butte and the chill of the spring air moved in on them.

The mare also laid back down to rest, tired from the foaling process. By sun up the following morning, the colt had taken on several fills of the rich, energy packed milk and was moving about quite well. His mother had rested and was able to really appreciate the new member of the herd, which she had just foaled.

He was a bay with quite a bit of white on his face; almost the whole nose area was white. He had four stocking legs. They were long, showing the thoroughbred breeding, almost to the point of looking too long for the rest of his body.

After a couple of days, the colt began running around, kicking up his heels and having fun. In doing so, he strayed away from his mother who was grazing, not watching his every move.

His every move *was* being watched however, by the stalking form of a coyote. Probably lured from Black Rock Butte by the smell of the new foal, this old coyote had decided to feed on the new born colt. As soon as the colt discovered the coyote, it's curiosity took over and he advanced towards the furry, dog like animal which looked like a fun thing to play with. As the coyote circled, trying to get closer to the colt, he passed a point where the air carried his scent directly to the mare. As the mother sensed the danger through her nostrils, her head was up and she went immediately to her new born colt with teeth bared and her ears laid back. She was ready for a fight. The old coyote, realizing he would be no match for the enraged mare protecting her young, retreated and went elsewhere looking for an easier prey.

On the third morning after foaling, the black mare went back to the mustang herd with her pride and joy at her heels. As they approached the other horses, the mare's foal from the last year came trotting out to meet them. She was a year old and stood much taller than her new born brother. she smelled him and looked him over trying to decide whether she liked the idea of him taking her place so close to her mother's side.

She gave him a little nip on the rump, but one look from her mother with her ears laid back made her realize that she would have to be good to the little fellow.

The summer passed swiftly for the wild colt, hardly giving him time to become familiar with the other live things on the Red Desert. Most of these were encountered and sniffed by the spring near Black Rock. There were other watering places too, but this was the main one.

The antelope were fun as they ran about checking the area for anything threatening to them. After deciding the area was all clear, they would proceed to the spring to drink.

Sage chickens would come in about sundown, usually flying to within 200 yards of the spring and walking from there to the water.

Mud turtles were a curiosity to the colts who would nudge them with their noses, sometimes striking them lightly with a hoof. The turtles would just pull into its shell and wait for the tormentor to go away. Horned toads, lizards and chipmunks are very quick to move away when approached.

The badger with its sharp claws and teeth earns respect in a hurry of almost all living creatures. They are built very close to the ground with very short, powerful legs.

As the horses watered at the spring, often another bunch would come to drink, waiting their turn until the first herd was done. After they had their fill, the first herd would usually leave the spring taking a trail leading out the opposite direction from which the waiting herd would approach the spring. This was the way they avoided conflict between the stallions. This is what we humans would call unwritten law or range courtesy.

The harem of the L Stud was alerted by one shrill whistle from the stallion as two large buck antelope ran swiftly past. something had spooked them and the stud was real quick to check for whatever had frightened them.

Suddenly a rider came into view, causing the mustang herd to move out quickly, each mare calling to her colt as they ran.

This was Slicker's first encounter with a human and he couldn't comprehend what all the commotion was about. He ran fast, following his mother's footsteps. He knew if she was frightened and running, there had to be a good reason. The black mare, leading the herd, headed north across a wide greasewood flat. A rifle shot was heard which only added to the fear and the intenseness of their flight. The sand hills to the north of them would help them get away if the rider followed. They were taking no chances and didn't slow down until they reached the sand hills. Slowing to a walk, they continued to the top of the first sand ridge. This is the way the colts learn to run and keep up with the herd, by running from anything that alarms them.

Looking back, they didn't see any riders so they continued walking while taking a much needed rest. They didn't know the rider was a hunter who bagged a nice buck antelope and wasn't interested in them at all.

Winter came to the Red Desert dropping a blanket of white snow on everything. Cottontail Rabbits scurried from bush to bush, looking for a small patch of bare ground to sit on while they fed on leaves. The Jack Rabbits didn't seem to mind the snow. They could run on the crusted snow on the high ridges.

The mustang colts had grown over summer; some nearly as tall as their mothers by now. When the cold raw wind blew, the mustangs moved into a deep brushy draw for protection. During a full blown blizzard, they would go into a deep wash, leaving a sentry on higher ground to watch for intruders. Slicker's mother took this position quite often, but the colt would remain in the wash among the other horses.

The snow came and covered the thin grass with the knee deep fluffy stuff. This wasn't to bad to paw out of the way for grazing. After a couple of days the sun came out bright, thawing the top just enough to make a thick crust on the snow when it turned cold again. This time it stayed cold for days, making it necessary for the adult horses to paw out the grass for the colts to graze on. Eating snow for water made it unnecessary for them to go the spring for water.

The welcome arrival of Spring found most of the horses in good shape. A few of the older mares and those nursing colts until late fall lost weight causing their ribs to show. As soon as the grass greened up in the spring they all put on weight and slicked off.

By the time Slicker shed his winter hair, he stood as tall as his mother. He was a beautiful long legged bay yearling stallion.

The followoing spring was Slicker's encounter with horse runners, which ended his freedom.

One morning we got up at the crack of dawn and wrangled the saddle horses. After the horses were fed oats, and we were fed sour dough pancakes and antelope chops we saddled up. Dad on a gray horse we called "Shorty," my youngest brother Sweed on "Queenie" a little bay mare and I was on a little powerful black we called "Pappy."

We followed a sage brush road that cut south through the sands then followed another almost straight east and eventually it cut southeast towards Black Rock Butte.

About five miles from the Butte we climbed to a taller knoll, one that was higher than the general terrain but not nearly as high as Black Rock.

We dismounted short of the knoll and went on foot to the top. Dad glassed the

Slicker

whole country side looking for a big bunch of mares and colts to run and try to corral. We only saw small bunches from this vantage point. A bunch of two or three usually meant young stallions that had been kicked out of the herd by the older stallion.

Dad waited here to be ready to relay on the way back if we were lucky enough to get a bunch back this far. Bill would ride out and be on a high knoll after the dishes were done. This would make him the last relay man. Sweed and I mounted and rode on towards Black Rock.

Dad had seen the L Stud and his band of mares and colts a few days earlier just north of Black Rock. The bunch had two light gray mares in it so it shouldn't be too hard to tell, if we would get a look at them. This country is rough and can hide many herds of horses, cattle and antelope.

About two miles farther, I left Sweed. He would ride on east about a mile because we were almost sure any bunch we would jump would try to go east towards the Red Strip. I kept on the trail towards Black Rock hoping to find a good bunch.

The sun was about a third of the way across the sky and was making the forenoon hot. I didn't find any horses before I got to Black Rock so Pappy and I had a cool drink from the spring. Just a couple of swallows though because a horse can't run on a full tank of water. Fresh horse tracks led up to the south from the spring. I picked my way among the soap holes that lay crusted and treacherous at the east side of the butte. I also spotted colt tracks in the trail and fresh manure on a stud pile about 20 yards off the trail.

We hadn't planned to cross Black Rock draw. It might be hard to bring the mustangs back across because the wash is pretty deep in a lot of places. The fresh horse sign looked pretty tempting to me so (cross it I did) in anticipation of finding a good sized bunch of mares and colts. It would be a lucky break to find the L̲ Stud and his bunch.

I rode on hoping that the next hill I topped would give me a look at a nice herd of horses. Looking back across Black Rock draw I could see Sweed off his horse, moving around quite a bit. I thought to myself, "he's probably catching horned toads, lizards or building a sheepherder monument out of flat rocks. I knew he'd have one eye on me.

The next little draw produced horses. Riding slowly, I topped the rise and when I saw them I quickly turned old Pappy around to a little lower ground. Tied to a sage bush he would wait while I had a good look see. My breath quickened as I took my hat off and just peeked the top of my head over the hill enough to see. At least the wind was from the west. This was in my favor because the horses were west of me about 600 yards. Wild horses have such a keen sense of smell I'm sure they can smell a human for a mile. (Not saying much for my hygiene, huh).

This was not the L̲ bunch and only seven or eight head, but I decided I would try them because to go much further would be too far and the horses over there fought real hard to go to the 12 mile rim. I'd have to get around to the southeast of them

Black Rock Butte

so I circled around leading my horse and being real careful not to make noise or to be seen.

As I reached the point from where I would start them, I took another look. If they'd run south I figured I could turn them and if they ran east I had a good open run on them that way. As I mounted old Pappy I had a kind of nervous excited feeling; the kind I used to get when I rode calves in rodeos in South Dakota a few years earlier.

The stud of the bunch saw me first and gave a shrill stud whistle and the race was on. They hit high speed in no time with tails and manes flying in the breeze. They were trying to go east but took off nearly straight north and were swinging back east. I started almost straight for Black Rock hoping to keep them west of the butte.

That stud gave me a ride for my money. I couldn't outrun him but he wouldn't leave the mares and colts and old Pappy could run the tails off the mares.

We were kicking up a real storm of dust by this time. I knew Dad would be watching with the glasses. Sweed was on the opposite side of Black Rock and probably was unaware of the action. The stud of the bunch had dropped back to the rear of the herd. A sleek black mare had taken the lead and was on a collision course with me. When she was about 50 yards away I hollered and she turned and headed northwest just the way I wanted her to. All I had to do now was beat her to the north side of the butte so I could keep her headed north till we got to Sweed.

I gave old Pappy his head. He knew what we had to do. Having been a wild stallion himself once, he was really adapted to this horse running and really loved it.

We hit the same trail that we had just came up on going full speed ahead. I couldn't see the bunch from here, they were on the opposite side of Black Rock from me. I had to go on the assumption that they would keep running north although they could easily turn west or back south.

Old Pappy hit the trail between the soap holes. I had visions of us being one big splat in the mud and bog. We didn't stop at the spring for a drink this time. It was full speed until we topped the ridge on the north side of Black Rock draw. The wild bunch had crossed at about the same time, but had headed northwest which was fine. At this point Sweed showed up a little ahead of me to take up his position in the chase. I reined Pappy in and let him trot to get a little breather. It would have been good to stop, but I had to keep up with the show.

The bunch had headed almost due west by this time and I cut northwest straight for Bill's place. Sweed followed the wild bunch afraid that they would go back across Black Rock Draw but the wash gets really deep and with the pressure that Sweed kept on them they weren't taking any chances on being caught in a dead end wash out.

The country is rough and at times I couldn't see the wild bunch or Sweed. Usually I could see the dust though. As I rode along at a brisk trot I saw a red fox go over a little knoll. This was the only fox I saw in Wyoming in the six years I lived out there. There were plenty of coyotes and badgers.

When I topped the next little rise, I could see that the wild bunch had picked up another herd in one of the swales when they were out of sight from me. I couldn't tell how many because they were a couple of miles from me, but they were strung out a long ways and kicking up a lot more dust. Unconsciously, I spurred my horse to a gallop wanting to be in on the action. I wanted to be there if we were lucky enough to corral them.

I eased off old Pappy though and walked him for a while. He had already had a fair work-out on the first heat. The cloud of dust continued on west for awhile then disappeared in a deep draw. The next thing I knew, Sweed was riding full speed nearly right towards me. Pappy saw him at about the same time as I did. His ears perked up and his breath quickened, he was ready to go.

The wild bunch had gone into the deep draw and had doubled back intent upon out-running Sweed and heading back for Black Rock Butte or possibly even the Red Strip where they would be safe. There was a well used wagon road down the draw that they were traveling in. This was to their advantage, they wouldn't have to dodge sage brush and rocks.

I was in a good position to try to head them off though, so I worked my way over to a spot where I could see them without being seen. I didn't watch for long as they were really moving. When they were about 600 yards away, I made my move. I rode at an angle towards them hollering and waving my hat. They kept coming down the road. Sweed was almost up to me, coming down the same ridge I had waited on. We should be able to turn them by working together.

Trying to count horses as I rode I guessed there were 18 or 20 head of grown horses. The colts were engulfed in dust. No way of telling how many there were. Sweed and I both knew we were in trouble when from the rear of the herd came a fleet footed powerful bay stallion really making knots. He was taking the lead, not trusting any mare to lead when the chips were down.

Well lead he did, darned near ran over me when he passed. I believe I could have reached him with a lariat but hadn't ever gotten it down.

As he whistled past me I could see the L branded on his jaw. I just had the feeling that we were being had by the L Stud.

The mares cut behind me to follow the stud but Sweed was still on that side of them and could still out-run the mares. I pulled up a little and let them all go by. No use splitting the bunch. Then I pulled alongside the bunch and rode flank for Sweed.

He was doing real well and was able to get ahead of the mares, but that stud came back into the bunch and outran Sweed, and the mares cut behind him. By this time I was up far enough to challenge the leaders. The mares were really tired and turned off the road and up over the ridge to the north. This was what we wanted if we only had horse enough under us to keep them headed that way. By the time we topped the ridge, the lead mare and I were neck and neck and there sat Dad on Shorty, fresh and full of spark. You could almost see defeat on the face of that lead mare as she was easily turned towards the sand hills and Steamboat Bill's place.

Sweed caught up to me shortly and we walked along and led our two very tired horses. We would let them rest awhile then head towards the corral. We wouldn't try to keep up but would be on hand in case they broke back again.

Dad pushed them pretty hard so they wouldn't get their second wind. They made almost a straight bee-line to where Bill was on a horse he called Brown Jug. Bill found himself in somewhat of a predicament because the bunch was headed straight towards him on a ridge that led up to the knoll where he sat. To stay out of sight of the wild horses he had to move around the north side of the hill which put him between the bunch and the corral.

After they had gone past him he headed about southwest trying to get around them. When they saw him they put on a new burst of speed. The L Stud left the bunch again and tried to draw the mares away but they were getting pretty tired and Brown Jug was a strong horse, raised in the sand where they were running now, so he soon overtook them. By the time Bill got them turned, they had run about 3 miles past the corral, towards the tables. Dad had reined Shorty to a stop as soon as Bill had taken over and was giving him a much needed breather.

Sweed and I had kept moving slowly towards the corral and had been able to see most of the running that had taken place. By the time we got up to where Dad was, Bill had turned the bunch back and they were heading nearly due east. Dad said, "Jack your horse has had the most rest so you go a little south and get ahead of them."

I went down a little draw keeping out of sight until I knew I had gone far enough then slowly looked over the ridge until I saw them. They were closer than I had expected. The long-legged mare was still leading the herd, her long tail floating in the breeze, her mane flying, she was determined once more to out-run old Pappy. She didn't get the job done though and with the help of Dad and Sweed, with Bill bringing up the rear, we headed them right towards the corral where my little sister, Jean, was holding the day herd in the wings. Most of the wild horses ran right in among our more gentle horses, who instantly headed into the corral.

One exception was the L Stud, he spotted one wing of that corral and darned near ran over Dad getting out of there. He was a beautiful sight, standing on a hill about a quarter of a mile away, calling to his harem who had yielded to the horse runners and were securely closed behind heavy pole gates. We got Slicker out of this herd. He wasn't named Slicker until we had him for awhile. I saw the stud a couple of times after that and he had about six or eight mares so I'm sure he was happy again and probably free forever.

The Coal Miner From Superior

I don't know where Dad met the coal miner from Superior, but he went to work for him. Don and Short went to work there too, and I joined them when school was out. The Miner had sent them down to Twelve Mile Spring to tear down and move a corral that was there. They had most of it moved to Coal Spring when Frank Robbins showed up at Twelve Mile. He was steaming mad because the corral happened to belong to him. The miner hadn't made this known to Dad so it was a real sticky situation for awhile.

The horse camp was set up near the natural corrals, east of Superior. There were two tents set up near a good spring of water. The wild horse corral was used for holding the saddle horses at night. One side of the corral was a big sandstone wall raising above the corral about 75 feet. The corral consisted of three separate pens so it could still be used for the gentle stock when we had wild ones in it.

By the time school was out and I got out there, the gentle bunches had all been gathered and they were going down around Black Rock Butte. The horses were wild down there and there were very few branded ones.

Excitement was running pretty high within me as we bounced along in the coal miner's pickup truck. The road was rocky and washed out in places as we crossed the ridge east of Superior. Dad and the miner were talking about some of the bunches they had caught and it sounded like fun to me.

Arriving in camp after dark, I didn't see much but a triangular shape of light which showed through the tent flap. As we walked towards the light I could hear a trickle of water of the small stream nearby. There was also a horse nicker, this would be old Pappy. The little black seemed to be hooked on oats and would always beg for a little when anybody was around. It was unbelievable how a horse could run wild for eight years and turn out as gentle as this one. We never hobbled him after

The coal miner on Silver, me on Casey, Dad on Shorty and Short on the coal miner's Slicker.

about the first month. He was always near camp in the morning. He was known as a good camp horse.

The smell of freshly cooked coffee came from the tent flap as we got closer to the tent. Don had stayed in camp and had made a pot, so we could enjoy a cup before turning in for the night. We planned the strategy for the wild horse chase for the next day before going to bed. Short would ride Slicker (a black horse belonging to the coal miner). He would take the long run. Then Don would be next on Buck. I was to ride Casey, a horse of the miner's also. His horses were all strange to me. I had never seen them so I was eager to get outside in the daylight for a look around. Dad would be on Shorty, and last and next to the corral would be the coal miner on his favorite horse, Silver.

I woke up the next morning to the sound of Dad yelling, "Come and get it." This was a welcome sound so I quickly got up, slipped on my Levis and boots and headed for the stream to wash up. It didn't take many splashes of that cold spring water to be enough.

Just after breakfast, we saddled up and headed east. The horse that Short rode was real touchy and we had to mess with him quite a lot. First, he didn't want the saddle on. Then he didn't want Short on his back. We finally convinced him that this was the only way to go. The miner led him about a dozen steps and away he went just like the rest of the saddle horses.

Taking a sheep camp road, we climbed up out of the canyon. The coal miner took his position where the road reached the top of the ridge. From this vantage point he could see the whole area for miles. Dad stopped off on a little knoll about a mile and a half farther down. The next post was mine. I was on lower ground but I was supposed to keep the wild horses from going down into Dead Man Canyon. Short and Don rode on over the next ridge out of sight of me in a short time. There wasn't anything to do now but wait and hope they bring a nice herd of mustangs my way.

As I sat there on a rock, I sized up the brown gelding that I had thrown my saddle on. He was a raw boned horse with a big head and big feet, a homely horse, to say the least. He wasn't lazy though and reined good. I figured he could run all day in the shade of an apple tree. The time passed slowly for me, partly due to the fact that I couldn't see very far in any direction. I figured, I got this old horse to ride just because I was a kid.

The sun was bright and there wasn't any wind, so I got real comfortable. While I was nearly at the point of dozing off, old Casey was being alert. The reins gave a jerk in my hand as he threw his head up to have a better look. This brought me to my feet, and sure enough there was a wild bunch headed right towards us. Not daring to get on my horse, I led him over the closest little hill and then mounted up. Old Casey was ready to go. I could tell this old horse loved to run wild horses.

Just about the time the leader was one hundred yards away, I popped out from behind the little knoll where I had been hiding, and the race was on. There was a sorrel mare in the lead and I could see that she didn't want to turn towards the corral. They were headed straight for Dead Man Canyon where I was supposed to keep them from going. This was about the time that I began having second thoughts about the quality of my mount.

This old brown horse was stretched out and really moving. The lead mare began to bend a little. The old stud of the bunch couldn't stand this so he hurried up and took the lead. As a rule, one of the older mares will lead and the stallion will bring up the rear, biting any stragglers on the rump to make them keep up. They usually take the lead when the going

One side of the corral was a sandstone wall.

gets tough. Old Casey and I were neck and neck with this stud when we busted over the rocky rim of the canyon. The wild bunch didn't slack off. They headed for the bottom at full speed. Old Casey didn't slack off either. We were just as determined to turn them as they were not to be turned.

As we got near the bottom, the stud veered off to the right. This was the right direction. I was in luck. The next second was a nightmare for me, because I hadn't been watching anything but the beautiful running stallion. There is something about these wild ones born free and taking advantage of everything that Mother Nature has to offer. They are always more beautiful with their sleek coats and long flowing manes and tails.

Just as the wild bunch turned, old Casey gathered himself and I knew he was going to jump. A quick look showed me a washout that somehow resembles the Grand Canyon. I just knew he wouldn't make it. I loosened up in the saddle so I

I figured the old horse could run all day in the shade of an apple tree.

could be thrown free if he took a bad spill. Where this homely old horse got the strength to jump this huge washout, I'll never know. But, after faltering just a little when he landed on the other side, we were soon at full speed again.

The wild bunch was running down Dead Man Canyon looking for a place where they could safely cross the washout. I turned Casey west down the canyon and began yelling like a wild man. The stud finally gave up trying to cross, and turned back up to go out of the canyon. As they nearly reached the top, Don was waiting for them and kept them in the rough breaks of the canyon. After a couple of miles of this, they reached Dad so Don let them come up out of the canyon.

The wild bunch was in the corral the next time I saw them. The washout in the bottom of Dead Man had been deep all the way out to the end of the canyon. I took my time and made a safe crossing this time.

I had learned a couple of good lessons that day. One, to always watch ahead when running horses in strange territory. The other, a fine example of the old saying "you can't judge a book by it's cover." This homely brown horse could run like the wind, jump like a deer and had a heart equal to anything I've ever seen.

The summer went quickly for me and when fall came, we moved to Superior to be closer to the wild horse operation. Superior was a coal mining camp with two or three working underground minds. Most of the town, including the mines, was owned by the Union Pacific Railroad. This and other surrounding camps furnished coal to fire their locomotives. Don and Short both worked in the D.O. Clark mine for awhile. Short didn't stay there very long.

Dad set out a trap line which he ran on horseback most of the winter. He began getting sick about Christmas time and got real thin. The doctor couldn't seem to put a finger on the trouble, but said it looked like he wouldn't make it till spring.

On March 3, 1941, Dad was struggling to throw a pack on a horse. He said he was going to the Coal Spring Camp in the desert. He said he enjoyed it out there and if he was going to die, he would go in peace out there. Don and I went into a huddle and decided that I should go with him. Don would stay on at the mine and bring out groceries and other supplies on his first day off. Dad tried to talk me out of going. He said I should finish school, he said my mother would have wanted me to, but I wasn't listening. I was too busy saddling up and putting a few personal items in a bag to take along.

The trip to Coal Spring was long and we took it real slow. Neither of us talked much, we were probably both thinking about the same thing. I wondered what it would be like to be with someone when they died. That was a bridge to be crossed when I came to it. The sun was bright and there was no wind, so it was an ideal day for a good long horseback ride. The snow was thawing good at mid-day but had reached the freezing point again as we drew near the camp. The sun had set on a clear horizon promising a nice day for the following day.

I had to help Dad into the tent, then I brought the bedroll inside and made the bed. He wanted me to rub his legs with absorbine, a strong liniment that we used for horse rub-downs after long runs. I did this after I got a good fire going in the stove.

Dad went to bed without eating hardly a thing. I ate enough for both of us, as I was nearly starved after riding all day. The old bedroll looked good to me too, and I was in it after I cared for the horses and cleaned up the dishes.

The weeks to follow were quite uneventful. Dad began feeling better and started getting his strength back. He didn't ever go back to the doctor, but he always said that it was the gas from the coal mines that nearly killed him off. By the time spring arrived we were ready to run wild horses again.

The Half & Half

It was one of those early summer mornings on the Red Desert. The temperature was ideal at this early hour, with the sun just breaking the horizon. I had gone out to wrangle the saddle horses that I knew would be within a mile of our wild horse camp.

We had finished our corral near Coal Spring Draw, southeast of Black Rock Butte, late in the fall before, and were real eager to run our first wild bunch into it. I walked along a horse trail headed east from camp carrying a nose bag filled with oats, to easily catch one of our saddle horses when I found them. The first horses I saw were about 1/2 mile from camp. Looking towards the sun I couldn't see them very well, but decided they weren't our saddle horses. There weren't enough of them and, besides, there were two little colts.

Deciding to have a look-see, I began looking for a way to get close to them without being seen. There was a shallow washout in the little draw. It wasn't deep enough to hide me but the sage brush was a little taller on both sides of it. This was the only possibility I could see, so I made my way over to it and began to work my way closer in the same manner that a hunter would stalk game. Part of the way I could stand up without being seen but other times I would go on my hands and knees. Slow and easy was the name of the game, because I didn't want to spook them out before I had gotten a good close look.

Occasionally, I would stop and peek over the brush for a look. There was one gray or white one. It looked like the stud standing off to the right. He was a brown horse, not very big, but sleek and shiny, really a beautiful sight. He'd look good under my saddle if I could ever catch him. Day-dreaming on, I kept getting closer, wanting to have a close look at them. The white one was probably an old gray turned white with age. The next look I got was pretty close, but there was a chestnut between the white one and me. I could only see the back half, so

93

back on my hands and knees for another 50 feet. This would soon have to end because the breeze would be blowing from me to the wild bunch. The gig would be up then because they would smell me.

Knowing this was as close as I'd get to them, I stood up. They saw me immediately and the stud gave a shrill whistle (the kind that only a wild stallion can give) and came closer to me for a good look. He also was curious.

The rest of the herd bunched up, the mares calling their colts close to them. At this time, I decided to have a good look at the white one but got the surprise of a life-time to discover there was no white one. What I had been seeing, thinking it was two horses, was one horse, one-half white and the other half chestnut.

About the time I had made this discovery, the old stud took out on a dead run, and the whole bunch went over the hill in a cloud of dust.

I ran most of the way back to camp very excited and eager to tell Dad and my brothers what I had seen. My chore of wrangling saddle horses had been momentarily forgotten in the excitement.

The next time I saw the half and half was about six days later. I was riding full speed after a bunch that we had started over close to the Sand Hills about straight north of Black Rock. We had run them about ten miles and they were pretty tired. I was riding wide on them so the colts could keep up.

They went into a little draw. I couldn't see the mustangs but could tell by the dust that they were still headed the right way. Pretty soon the dust thickened and speeded up. I knew what had happened and cussed a little bit. They had run into a fresh bunch and were really moving out. Luckily, they kept on in the direction that would take them to Dad, who was on a hill just south of Black Rock Wash. He was our last relay man and it looked like he would have his hands full if he was to head them into the wings of our corral.

I hadn't seen the fresh bunch yet, but kept watching the dust until they came out of the draw and broke over the ridge into Black Rock Draw.

Jack on Rusty.

When that half and half saw me, he practically flew. Luckily, he seemed content to keep on in the direction that we wanted him to go. That whole bunch of fresh horses was a fast moving outfit and were soon quite a ways ahead of the bunch that we had been chasing.

They approached Dad at full speed, but he stayed hidden until the fast bunch, with the half and half in it, was pretty well past him. Then he rode out and, after quite a run, was able to turn the tired bunch and we initiated our corral with a fine bunch of mustangs.

I was pretty disappointed that Dad didn't try to get the bunch with the half and half. He explained later that we would have probably lost all of them if we would have tried to corral them altogether because the tired ones would be strung out so far that the lead ones would be coming back out of the corral before the tail-enders ever got there.

There were eleven head in the bunch that we got. One of them was Rusty, a two year old sorrel stud, that turned out to be one of my favorite saddle horses.

It seemed that the half and half disappeared after that. We would go out to specially look for his bunch, but would end up taking a different bunch. We had good luck running to the Coal Spring Corral. Of course, we spilled a lot of bunches, too.

We spent most of the summer there, but as fall drew near, too many horses knew where our corral was and we couldn't get them near it.

Shorty

Short had worked for Jim Ramsay for a year and was staying at the ranch doing chores while Jim was away.

Jim, Doyle Saglauske, Bill and Paul Williams were running horses in the Marshes and Greasewood country between Little Mountain and Green River. The wild horse population was on the increase so they decided to thin it out a bit. They rode this country often and watched the horse herd closely. They knew of several young stallions which would be good saddle horse material, if they were lucky enough to catch them.

They evidently had good luck because Jim gave Short a little gray stallion. Jim was already calling the four year old mustang Old Short, so the name stuck but we called him Shorty. It was early spring when Jim gelded him. I don't know if the cold nights had anything to do with it but he swelled up real bad so Jim turned him out east of the ranch, next to the McGath butte.

We hadn't seen him for several days so Dad asked if I would walk up on the butte to see if I could locate him. Short was busy at Ramsays and wouldn't have the time to go himself. I walked along a ridge which would take me to the heads of several deep draws. As I walked the ridge each draw would become visible to me. As I came upon the third draw I spotted Shorty at about the same time as he saw me. He snorted and threw up his head and tail. He started to run away but I'm sure the pain of his recent operation prompted him to stop. I was sorry I hadn't been careful, so as to not spook him. This had to hurt. Upon my return to the ranch, Dad assured me the horse would probably be all right. He said it had been long enough since the operation that the infection was probably on it's way out. We watched him progressively heal up, fatten and really slick up as he shed his winter coat.

Short broke him to ride that summer under the watchful eye of Jim, who I'm sure gave him many helpful pointers. This little horse, weighing about 900 pounds, developed into a super saddle horse. He was an easy riding horse with an easy lope that could carry a man all day and yet have a good burst of speed when it was needed.

Dad always enjoyed riding Shorty. Having been broke working cattle, he reined exceptionally well. He wasn't a tall horse which made mounting him easy. Dad said he was a good "Old man's horse."

Dad trapped during the winter months. Riding trap lines was tiring work, requiring much getting off and on so Dad particularly favored Shorty for this job. It was quite common to get snowed on while running the trap line. Dad was going abut his business of checking one trap after the other during a light snowfall which was rapidly changing into a hard snowfall. By the time he was done checking the traps, the wind had come up and the temperature had plummeted. As he started towards the camp the driving snow was stinging his face so badly he soon had to cover it almost completely and soon became disoriented. Not realizing he was mixed up he rode on. Shorty began to try to go in a direction which Dad figured was wrong. Dad fought him, forcing him to go where he wanted him to go, finally to discover he had crossed his own path and was going in circles. That was when he gave Shorty his head. Covering up as well as he could, he just rode. As he rode he was thinking; "what if the little mustang decides to take me to his home range, about seventy miles away? Because the railroad was fenced, he would have to cross the Union Pacific track in a town, probably Point of Rocks or Rock Springs. Those are twenty five to thirty five miles away. More than likely Shorty will go to the horse camp."

I'm sure many things ran through Dads mind as he put his life in the judgment of this little horse. With the density of the storm, darkness was moving in swiftly adding to the hopeless feeling which had swept over Dad since he discovered he had lost his sense of direction.

I had stayed in camp to tend to the other horses and the dogs. It was my job to have supper ready when Dad returned. I had boiled potatoes and fried a cottontail rabbit we got the day

Shorty

before. I'd leave the gravy for Dad to fix; there seemed to be a lot less lumps that way.

The storm raged on, violently shaking the tent so hard that I wondered if it could withstand the force. Also concerning me was the fact of darkness closing in and Dad not returning yet. The warm light of the lamp gave me a good secure feeling but still there was a gut feeling that something might have happened to him. I thought of firing three times in the air with a high powered rifle, but with that much wind, the sound wouldn't carry very far.

Dad rode for what seemed like an eternity, not daring to get off the horse. He was too stiff and too cold to get back on. No need to walk he didn't know which way to go. The snow was getting deeper and Shorty walked slowly. When he came to a stop, Dad figured he was tired and tried to urge him on. Shorty wouldn't move. Dad finally peered out against the storm and saw a sliver of light. Shorty had stopped right in front of the tent with the light shinning through the crack where the flap fastens. Dad called to me and I untied the flap, letting him inside where he warmed up while I put Shorty away. Shorty was treated to an extra measure of oats that night!

Dad said he'd always heard "if you give a horse his head he will take you home." It is awfully hard to do as long as you think you know where to go, but when you lose your sense of direction, you have no choice.

Wild Horse and Barbed Wire

Barbed wire is one of the horse's worst enemies. Very few gentle horses go through life without a scar or two if they spend much time in and around barbed wire fences.

You might see a cow caught in the wire, jerking a leg that had become entangled in the barbs, finally getting loose, suffering only a minor scratch and the loss of a little hair, rubbed off in the struggle. But a horse in the same situation, would probably be cut clear to the bone or possibly into the bone. I have seen them wire-cut in a muscle or joint, leaving them deformed, stiff and therefore unusable for life. Barbed wire had no place in any wild horse corral I was ever around.

That was the one thing ranchers hated most about the early homesteaders. They brought the barbed wire which crippled and maimed many of their good horses.

On a recent trip to the Red Desert, we came upon the carcass of a horse, all tangled up in barbed wire. The remains had been there for quite awhile. Not much was left but barbed wire and bones.

The story was easy to read as Sweed and I traced the wires. Some of them encircled the leg bones several times. The horse had become tangled in it, fought it but couldn't get loose and eventually died. We can only speculate as to whether he bled to death, got infection or just how death came but barbed wire was definitely the main cause for it's death.

The only other barbed wire we saw on the desert was at the twelve mile spring where the BLM had dug a well or re-located the spring. The water is partially fenced off where it runs out of a pipe into a pond. One end of the pond is left open for access to animals watering there.

I don't understand the purpose of the fence, but my thinking is; as long as wild horses watered there, unbothered, there would be no problem. However, if something was to spook them, they could easily run through the fence, getting badly cut and possibly become entangled in the barbed wire.

Open wounds become infected causing blood poisoning which in turn draws flies who are always looking for a place like this to lay their eggs. The fly eggs eventually turn into maggots, making a real mess out of an already open sore. Out on the desert, the horse would go unnoticed and without medical attention, it would be almost sure to die.

The Red Desert

Wyoming's Red Desert fits to a "T" the dictionary's definition of desert; a dry, sandy area with little or no vegetation, especially wild and uninhabited. With these facts in mind, it is hard to imagine it's being anything but dull, with hardships at every turn. This would be the impression gathered by the ordinary person traveling across the state from east to west or vice versa. Only the ones who take the time to become involved in nature's wonders of the desert are the ones who learn to enjoy the strange beauty of the seemingly barren land.

The sugary white sand dunes are definitely a fascinating attraction. They change shapes as the changing winds drift the fine sand into ridges and peaks, hollowing out many places where a hill had been. In time, the snow melting from within the sand will form a lake in it's place. the sand dunes extend into the desert for approximately thirty or forty miles.

Near the sands, petrified turtles, snails, sponges, and oyster beds have been found. Fossil fish can be found on some of the higher ridges bordering the desert. Across the desert, there appears much evidence of volcanic action taking place centuries ago. To the west is the largest of these, Steamboat Mountain. Named so because of it's image like that of a huge ship, the southern most part of the mountain forms the bow out of rounding lava rock cliffs.

The near by tables, with their flat tops have intrigued many a person to climb them. Included among those was a fellow who came to the Chilton ranch while I was there. He said he was a Geologist, interested in the Red Desert and what it had to offer in the line of information. He had been fascinated by the tables and had climbed the tallest of them. He had done this in the heat of this summer day, without taking any water with him. He was about done in and could hardly wait to be shown inside the spring house at the Hooten place. He took the dipper from my hand, dipping it into the cold spring water in

Steamboat Mountain
Bill Lewis place was just below where the skyline makes a V in upper left.
Note white sand dunes in middle of picture.

one swipe. He began drinking very fast, spilling it down his chin in his haste. He began to weave back and forth. I thought he would collapse and fall into the spring. I advised him to drink slower and not to over do it. He did slack off, but sat around there for most of an hour, taking short drinks until his thirst was completely quenched. He then climbed into his car and headed out, in a cloud of dust, in the direction of Rock Springs.

The Boar's Tusk is located west of the tables and Steamboat Mountain. It too is a lava rock formation. The name fits the rock, as it stands up from the desert floor very much resembling a boar's tusk. Looking to the south, the Leucite Hills can be seen on the skyline, marking the place where the coal mining town of Superior is hidden in a deep canyon. Black Rock Butte and Spring Butte are to the east and north of Superior. These are all lava rock formations.

A spring of good water trickles out of the butte so aptly named, Spring Butte. Black rock also has a spring in the draw near by. A short distance east of this butte is a small flat which is loaded with treacherous soap holes. Livestock often get into them and suffocate or drown in the murky muddy water. they are so dangerous because they appear to be dry on the surface, but under the dry crust is a hell hole of mud. Dad and I pulled a mustang out of a soap hole once. His head, shoulders, and front feet were above the mud as he struggled for his life. His tail end was almost straight down, as if he had fallen into a well. We put our lariats on him, pulling, struggling and finally pulling him free. The cement like mud stuck to his hair all summer. He was tired out from the struggle for his life. He spent a lot of time laying in the sun for a few days.

Very fragile is the way to describe plant life on the desert. Delicate root systems fight an unending battle to support it. Even the sage, as rough and tough as it appears takes what seems like forever to become reestablished, once it's root system has been destroyed. With top soil restricted to small clumps, we have to wonder how anything got started in the first place.

Spring brings out the beauty of plant life on the desert. Cactus blossoms and desert roses are of the more delicate ones to look at, but try to pick a bouquet and you will surely get thorns in your fingers. Wyoming's state flower, the Indian Paint brush, is found on many of the higher ridges. The many varieties of brush also take on pretty colors. Rabbit Brush is a yellow green, while sage brush has a purple tint to the green, giving off a pungent, but otherwise indescribable aroma which you almost become addicted to. Greasewood, the main source of salt in the diet of the animals, is colored a beautiful green. It too is thorned by nature for protection from the ravages of every day living in such surroundings.

Creatures, such as horned toads and sand lizards, are well camouflaged as they slither across the rocks and sand to a safe hiding place. Scorpions are under many loose rocks, with their stinger up for anyone trying to intrude upon them. Chipmunks scurry away quickly if they sense danger. If you get the opportunity to pick one up, be prepared, because they are scrappy little fellows with sharp teeth and claws.

The howling of coyotes has been the lullaby for putting wranglers to sleep probably ever since there have been wranglers. There is something to be said for the soothing sound as you snuggle down into the bed on the wide open spaces. After a hard day in the saddle it doesn't take long to be lulled to sleep. My joy was always enhanced by the sound of young coyotes. In the spring of the year they would emerge from the den staying quite close to the hole under the close surveillance of the mother, who usually didn't spend much time in the den except to feed the pups. She normally could be seen sitting on a high knoll where her keen sense of sight and smell looked after the welfare of her litter. As the pups grew towards maturity, they would follow their parents to a high knoll where they would join in the howling at night. Singing off key in their immature voices, they were very easy to distinguish from the mature coyotes. By the time winter blankets the ground with snow, they have matured enough to blend right in with the old timers.

Badgers are probably the same the world over. Seems as if they prefer to dig holes right in the middle of a hard packed road or trail. The Red Desert is home to many badgers, digging their deep holes everywhere. they are seldom seen in the day time, but their presence is evidenced in the form of freshly dug holes. The first visible part of the burrow is the pile of dirt. The size of the piled depends on how deep the hole is. These holes are seldom stepped in by mustangs, who are smart enough to know where there is a mound of dirt there is likely to be a hole. Occasionally a badger will dig a shallow tunnel. A horse on the run breaking through and stepping into one of these is likely to take a spill.

With the coming of the first snow, begins the turning of color of the jack rabbits. their furry coat turns white as the snow. They are given this by nature, as protection from predators. Cotton tail rabbits retain their brownish gray color, winter and summer. They rely on their quick departure to take them safely down a hole.

An oddity among the creatures of the desert is the kangaroo mouse. Carrying himself in almost an upright position, he travels on long stout hind legs. carrying his shorter, much smaller front ones almost limply in front of him. They travel in much the same manner as their name sake, the kangaroo. They also have a long stout tail, which they use extensively in travel. It adds balance to the almost deformed looking body. The tail also is used as a support.

Bluebirds abound, being probably the prettiest of the birds of the desert. Others often seen are, magpies, black birds and an occasional meadow lark.

Sage chickens were plentiful around most of the springs, raising their broods near the water for their survival. the young chickens are tender and very tasty, but try an old one. You'd be as well off to eat your boots. The old ones are identifiable by their black plumage on their breasts.

The magpies are pretty birds, black and white, with a slim body and long tail. Their diet includes meat. Their specialty is riding around on a sore backed horse, picking away at the sore. For this reason they aren't considered a favorable bird.

This is the way the old desert was when we were on it. I'm sure it hasn't changed a whole lot since.

Home Made Hand-Me-Down Chaps

"Let 'er buck!" was the call from Short as Chuck and Don turned the calf loose with him on it's back. He didn't stay on long even though the chaps my brothers had fashioned from a pair of dish towels, shanghaied from Mamma's clothes line when she wasn't looking, were supposed to give him a professional edge. This didn't seem to be the case and Short was soon picking himself up and dusting the corral dust off his clothes. It was late in the evening when Mamma discovered her dish towels gone and found out what they had been used for. By this time her sense of humor had completely vanished and she could see nothing funny about this episode. She laid down the law. There would be no more items taken from the clothes line without her permission.

Dad was away on a horse trading trip at the time, but when he got back he was properly informed by Mamma and he too gave a pep talk about how things should run smoothly around the place when he was away.

His next horse trading trip took him west-river to the Cheyenne River Indian Reservation.

Dad took three used Model T Fords along to trade for horses. They were all black. I believe at that time the choice of colors was black or black, however one of them had been repainted and looked better than the other two. Mamma asked Dad why he didn't keep this shiny good looking one and take along the one we had used for several years as trading stock. He said our old one was much better mechanically and would give us a lot better service than the one that looked shiny and new.

Don and Short got to go with Dad on that trip. chuck stayed home to help Mama with chores. As for me, I was too young to go trading horses or to do much at home either.

Speed Martinez, Chuck and Jack wearing homemade chaps. Chilton's corral on Steamboat Mountain.

Time dragged for me while they were gone. Dad had written a couple of letters and had apparently told Mama when to expect him home. She hadn't let that be known to us because things didn't always go as scheduled with the broncos, some of them very wild and some broke horses among them.

Mama's eyes had been scanning the western horizon all day, watching for a wisp of dust being stirred up by the horses and wagons on the dry prairie road. Sunset was upon us. Darkness enveloped us and she hung the lighted lantern on the porch to serve as a beacon if they should be late getting home. About ten o'clock, the moon came up big and bright, making it possible for them to ford the Jim river which bordered our place on the west.

After the horses were all put away we talked and listened. Dad did most of the talking with Don and Short telling about some of their adventures, such as helping round up horses on the Indian Reservation. they had gone to LaPlant, Eagle Butte, White Horse and Cherry Creek. Even the names of these towns sounded exciting to me.

On this trip they had traded for two shetland ponies. A bay and white spotted one and a black. The spotted pony was taller than the black so they were named Mutt and Jeff. Jeff, the taller one was also a good kids pony. He was mild mannered and gentle, but that Mutt would bite, kick and strike if he got the chance. He mellowed some as the older boys rode him but he didn't become trustworthy and was soon trading stock.

Dad had also acquired some leather on the reservation. This was to be used in making chaps for his bronc riding kids. He had gotten a buckle for the belt and snaps for the legs. The leather tanned by the Indians was soft, pliable, and easy to work with. Mom and Dad both worked on the chaps, doing a nice job on our first real pair of bronc rider chaps. They were far too big for me but were handed down from Chuck to Don, to Short and then to me, then to Sweed. I'm not sure if the chaps really enhanced our riding ability but they seemed to cling to the saddle leather a bit better than blue denim did. At any rate, it stopped the snitching of towels from the clothes line, while still allowing the riding of anything that would buck, to continue.

I grew into the chaps about the time we moved to Wyoming. They were good protection to my legs while riding through tall brush and thick stands of Cedar trees.

Soon after we arrived at the McGath place on Trout Creek, I was invited to help the local ranchers with the sorting of cattle. Jimmy Ramsay, Jack Logan and I rode to the Harris place together. The ride was probably five or six miles to the north from our place. The Harris place belonged to the Gottschie Ranches.

It was late in the Fall and the operation would consist of separating the calves from their mothers for weaning. A few of the calves had been missed during the branding roundup so they were branded along with the weaning. The cattle were being held on a peninsula of land surrounded on three sides by the washed out banks of Sage Creek. The banks dropped straight down ten or more feet which served as a corral on three sides, leaving only one side to be guarded by riders.

Jim Ramsay and Bill Logan were roping the calves which needed branding. They were branded, then turned loose in a corral. The calves were all put into one corral and the mother cows in another. Jack Logan, Jimmy Ramsay and I, along with a couple of Gottschie hands were holding the cattle on the side which required riders.

By the time the work was done, darkness had settled in on us. We unsaddled our horses and turned them into a corral, separate from the cattle. After feeding them hay and watering them, we proceeded to the house to feed ourselves. Sauerkraut and Weiners have never been my favorite, but they sure tasted good that night. We were all tired and turned in early.

There was no family living at the Harris place, just a few ranch hands. The older ranchers slept in the main house, leaving us younger hands to roll our blankets in the bunk house. The calves were in a corral which included the back side of the bunk house as part of the enclosure.

The calves, having just been weaned and some had a burning sensation on their side from the brand, were feeling really sorry for themselves and bawled all night. Consequently, we didn't get much sleep.

The wake up call came early and we were soon sitting at the long table in the dining room of the log ranch house. Those sour dough hot cakes were sure good, served with bacon and eggs and cooked to perfection.

By the time the sun came over the cedar covered hills east of the ranch we were saddled up and ready for the ride back home. Clouds soon moved in from the west and the sunshine disappeared. when we were about half way home a light drizzle began to fall out of the clouds. As we rode our horses along the trail through the Big Dry Hollow, we could tell we were in for a rain, possibly turning to snow.

We all had slickers tied to our saddles and we soon had them on. I was thankful for my home made chaps. They really turned the rain and kept me dry and warm.

By the time we arrived home it had turned colder and begun to snow. After unsaddling old Whitey, I turned him onto the hay meadow with the other horses. I went into the house to warm up while telling the rest of the family about my exciting week end which was a welcome break from school.

Capture of the Candy Horse

The spring in Coal Spring Draw was no more than a seep hole in Spring and by mid-summer it was completely dry. The water wasn't fit for human consumption so we hauled our drinking water from the spring at Black Rock Butte. We took the horses there to water every day. On extremely hot days they had to be watered twice. The canvas water bags hung easily, one on each side of the saddle and weren't any trouble if the horse just walked, but if he trotted, they sure bounced. The water stayed reasonably cool hanging in a shaded place in camp. The bags remained damp allowing the evaporation process to cool the water inside.

The day herd was allowed to graze to the spring at Black Rock, which was about three miles away. The horses would drink while we filled the water bags. After the horses had their fill of water, some of the older saddle horses would just automatically begin grazing their way back towards the camp. They knew they would be fed oats about sun down. Jean, Sweed and I were making one of these, rather boring, trips on a very hot and still day. The deer flies were bad on the horses and sure weren't above biting humans either. Jean was riding old Pappy and was afraid the little black might get to fighting flies and run with her. She was glad when we reached the spring where she could get her feet on the ground. While we were busily filling the water bags, Pappy's head jerked up, he had spotted a wisp of dust on the horizon to the north. In a few minutes four head of horses came to drink in the spring, about three hundred yards below where we had the day herd. There were no colts with them, causing us to believe they were young stallions. As we viewed them through the glasses, we saw one roan with stocking legs and a blaze face. This would be Dick's Candy horse. One was black, the other two were bay. The roan gelding was with three young studs. They would probably be a fast moving outfit when they got to running. We wanted that

112

roan horse to use but I didn't want them to get mixed up with our day herd because we had some freshly caught wild ones in there which we could easily lose if they decided to run and split up on us. We quickly decided that my horse, Old Appy, was the fastest runner, so I got between the four head, which included the Candy horse, and the day herd.

Jean and Sweed would return the day herd to camp, positioning them in the wings of the corral. I would try to bring the four head and run them into the day herd to be corralled. I led my horse to a position between the two bunches of horses, staying closer to the day herd so I wouldn't spook the four head. The smaller bunch kept eyeing the day herd while they drank. After they had their fill of water, they decided to take a closer look. Jean, Sweed and I mounted up at about the same time. The four head took off at a swift gallop back the direction from which they came. I figured they wouldn't go far if no one followed them, so I helped Jean and Sweed start the day herd towards the corral before following them. Following the same trail as the Candy horse and his companions had, I led old Appy to the top of the hill so I could have a look. They had slowed to a walk about 1/2 mile away, still headed north. The country is mostly open to the north of Black Rock, with a few draws and ridges reaching to the sand hills. I would have to ride quite far to get around them without being seen. Heading my saddle horse east down the wash, I rode to where the second draw came in. By riding in the bottom of this dry wash I could stay out of sight of the four head. There was no hurry, as it would take the day herd a good hour to travel back to the corral and get set to play the role of decoy. Making my way cautiously up the dry draw, I caught an occasional glimpse of the horses, they had stopped to graze on a small salt sage flat. As I got closer the draw became more shallow. I dismounted and led my horse to remain out of sight of the Candy horse and his companions.

The wash out passed close to the horses, increasing the danger of spooking them if my horse or I should make noise. About two hundred yards farther I ran out of cover so I mounted up again, much to their surprise. They all threw up their heads and tails as if they were show horses. They swiftly broke into a lope as they headed towards the tables. Riding wide to the right of them I gradually gave old Appy free reign, edging in a little on them so they would head more south. The black led with the candy horse bringing up the rear. Gradually they turned and headed south, just what I wanted them to do. As they got closer to the Black Rock wash, about two miles west of the butte, they began to crowd my way again. They didn't want to cross the wash and I could see there was going to be a horse race as they challenged me. The black could really run when he stretched out with his mane and tail flying in the wind. Old Appy could run too and it looked like it could be a tie race as we drew near the wash out in the bottom of the draw. The black could see it too and turned away to find a place to cross farther away from me.

After crossing the wash, they slowed to a trot headed in a southerly direction. I crossed the wash in the same place they did, crossings aren't too plentiful on the Black Rock wash.

Appy was glad for the slower pace, giving him a chance for a breather. Looking southeast I could see a small cloud of dust, this would be the day herd slowly making it's way towards the corral. They would have plenty of time to get set in the wings, but my concern was, would someone have time to ride out to help me? Old Appy was good for one more good run at them, but if I was lucky enough to turn the Candy horse and his bunch towards the corral, someone on a fresh horse would be a welcome sight. By this time the black stud had broken into a gallop. Appy was watching them as closely as I was. He automatically began to run pulling slightly to the right, so we could turn them southeast towards the corral. The black held a straight southeast course straight towards Deadman Canyon. The canyon breaks would quickly swallow them up and I would have to give up the chase if they made it into the rough country that makes up the canyon. Not knowing their intentions, I pushed on, hoping to be able to turn them before they reached the rim of the canyon. At this point the Candy Horse took the lead, breaking out in front with a great burst of speed. Surely he would lead them into the canyon. Just about the time

I figured they were gone, the Candy Horse turned east along the canyon rim. He followed the two track wagon road for about 1/2 mile then left it to head northeast back towards Black Rock. They were wasting no time, so I gave Old Appy his head as we also headed towards the butte. This would be an endurance race between four footloose horses and a grain fed saddle horse carrying a rider.

Full speed ahead we raced, rocks clattered under the shod hoofs of my faithful saddle horse. The Candy horse kept the lead but sweat was appearing ahead of his shoulders and in his flanks. He was slowly tiring and it wasn't necessary to look to know Appy was sweating too. The smell was strong in my nostrils. Soon he would have to slow down for a breather but we were getting closer to the corral. Had anyone come out to help? Looking into the general direction of the corral I located a dark spot on a low hill. It could be a rider's head, peeking over to watch the race and to be able to help when we got that far. Spurring Appy on for one last sprint, I headed right towards the spot on the hill, I knew this would be his last heat of the day. If the spot on the hill wasn't a rider, they would be back across the Black Rock wash in ten minutes and I would be headed into camp leading one tired horse. Suddenly the spot moved and came into plain sight as horse and rider took up the chase. Sweed had a good run at them. The Candy horse got almost within roping distance of him before turning towards the corral. Easing Old Appy to a slow canter, I rode straight toward the corral, arriving just in time to see the gate go shut on the Candy horse, his three companions and the day herd.

By this time, the shadows were growing longer, and by the time we had our saddle horses cooled and rubbed down, the old sun was slipping down behind Spring Butte. Evening on the desert is a beautiful time, growing cooler and very quiet as it gets dark.

We were up at dawn, there was branding to do and we were all anxious to see what we had corralled the day before. Hopefully, the wild ones would be settled down some. Sometimes, they get spooked and run into the corral and injure them-

Mike Redockovich in front of our tent at Coal Spring. Mike and his brother had come to buy horses.

selves, usually scratches and bruises, but occasionally one would break its neck. For this reason we didn't go near the corral after the gate was closed the night before.

The Candy horse was pretty and after looking him over, Dad pointed at his jaw. There's the reason Dick couldn't sell him or give him away. He had a worked over brand on his jaw. Dad dropped a loop on him. He snorted and jumped, but turned around and faced Dad. He acted as wild as the rest of them, but they never forget the rope after they have been halter broke. Dad worked his way up the rope, talking to him and finally patted him on the neck. The little horse seemed to loosen up and lose his fear as Dad worked with him.

Next, he was served a coffee can full of oats, which he ate like a kid eats candy. We saddled him, and three others, to ride to the spring. After the three young studs were branded and each had a front foot tied up, we let them out with the day herd to graze and to make their way to the spring for a drink. They soon discovered they couldn't run very well with a foot tied up. It sure made them easier to handle and to keep in the day herd.

Sweed and Jean handled the day herd nicely as Dad and I took our time with the Candy horse. We snubbed him to Dad's saddle horn while I got on him. He humped up his back but soon straightened out after he was led for about a quarter of a mile. We turned him loose then and he crow hopped a little with me but didn't buck hard. He was a sensible little horse, a good camp horse that needed no hobbles as long as he got oats every day. We used him alot, treating him just like we did our own horses. He wasn't a fast runner, but had good staying power and could run a long distance with a light rider on his back. Don was riding him the day he roped the half and half stallion.

By the time we left the desert, we had heard of Stutterin Dick's death, so we just turned the Candy horse out on the desert, hoping he would enjoy his freedom for the rest of his life.

Breaking Seal

The black mustang we had caught with the Candy horse, appeared to have the makings of a good saddle horse, so we decided to break him. He was a horse which weighed about 1,000 pounds, was narrow in front with high withers, a short back, rounded rump and long slim legs. The three year old had a well muscled body for his age. The pasterns were long, indicating he would have plenty of speed. All of these features set squarely upon four small and very well formed feet with hooves like iron. Anyone would be glad to have such a horse in their remuda. The small amount of brown blending in with his black hair is what prompted us to name him Seal.

Dad roped him by the front feet and with my help, was able to throw him down. Once he was down, Dad kept pressure on the rope, holding him down while I hurriedly got on his head. With the mustang's nose turned upwards with my knee securely in the bend of his neck, he stayed put while Dad tied his feet. With three of his feet tied together, his only option was cooperation. We put a heavy leather halter on him, looped a heavy soft-twist rope around his flanks, brought it forward under his belly, between his front legs, through the halter ring, and finally tying it to a good sturdy corral post. After branding him we took the rope off his feet, allowing him to get on his feet and to pull on the heavy rope. After rearing back violently several times, he finally eased up on it. Faced with the reality that he couldn't escape, he was soon leading by the halter rope, eating oats and in general, proving he was an intelligent animal. Seal would be gelded later in the Fall when the threat of flies was no longer present. Flies lay eggs in an open incision causing infection. If not treated properly, an animal will die from this infection.

The next step of the breaking process involved tying up a hind foot. This enabled us to do almost anything with the horse without harm to him or to the one doing the breaking. The foot

118

tying up, began with a large noose around Seal's neck, back towards the withers, draped over the left shoulder. This rope was also a heavy, soft twist rope to help eliminate rope burn if he struggled, which he was almost certain to do. The big noose around his neck was tied with a bowline knot so it wouldn't pull tight and choke the horse. The loose end of the rope was then worked between the hind feet, brought around the right foot, back under the horse's belly and through the noose. Before it was tightened it had to be positioned below the ankle, just above the hoof of the right hind foot. As the rope was quickly tightened Sealy became spooked and nearly fell down as the use of his right hind foot was taken away from him. When he had quit struggling, I took another wrap around his foot, securing it with a couple of half hitches. I checked to be sure the tied up foot was off the ground far enough so he couldn't get it on the ground, which would enable him to kick with the untied foot. Care had to be taken also to not tie it too high. This would be very uncomfortable to him, causing him to continually fight it. Next, I began to pat him softly with my hands, beginning at this neck and working back along his ribs, ending with his ticklish flank. Picking up the saddle-blanket with my right hand, taking the halter rope with my left, I moved slowly to his small, well shaped head where I allowed him to smell the blanket and to look it over real good. The old blanket had been on many horses since it had been laundered, so the odor of horse would be on it. The blanket was used to sack him out until most of the spook had left him, then I placed it upon his back where a saddle blanket belongs. By this time he had lost most of his fear of me and of what I was doing with him. The saddle was next. After allowing him to look it over and to smell it, I placed it gently but firmly on his back. He flinched as the stirrup and cinch dropped down along his right side. He didn't expect anything to move on that side of him.

Carefully I reached under and grabbed the cinch, threaded the latigo through the ring several times. Slowly, I drew the latigo strap pulling the cinch slowly but firmly up against his chest. He humped up his back just a bit as the cinch made contact with his chest. The rear cinch was pulled up so it just touched his belly, alerting him to the fact that it was there. The bridle is what he disliked most. We always broke horses with a snaffle bit. This straight bit with a hinge in the middle, was easy on the horse's mouth. This kept them from becoming cold jawed or hard mouthed, a condition which caused them to be hard to handle.

He didn't want the bit in his mouth. Finally, by putting pressure on his gums with my thumb in the space where he would be getting his bridle teeth in about two years, I was able to get him to open his mouth and accept the bit. He began chewing the bit immediately, which is normal for a horse that hasn't experienced the bit before. Seal began showing signs of being tired of standing on three legs. He had been handled enough for one day, so I reversed the whole procedure, taking everything off him and turned him loose in the corral. The first thing he did was roll in the loose dirt in the corral. He rolled completely over twice before rising up to shake the loose dirt off his sleek coat.

The old timers always said a horse was worth one hundred dollars for each time he rolled over. We figured we had quite a horse in that freshly captured mustang.

For the next couple of weeks, I devoted as much of my time as I could to working with this young stallion who seemed so willing to learn.

The next step in the breaking process consisted of saddling him, putting the bridle on and tying the reins tightly, first to the right, and after a half hour to the left, to a soft rope tied around the horse's flank. This teaches him to turn to the pressure on the reins allowing the rider to spin him out of a bucking pattern if he chose to bog his head and buck. This didn't always work, but as a rule it was a real advantage to the cowboy doing the breaking.

After about the third time I no longer tied his foot up. He was taming down real well. I had practiced mounting him by putting my foot in the stirrup with my weight on the saddle without getting all the way on him. To get all the way on would probably spook him, causing him to fall with his foot tied. After a few times he lost his spookiness, allowing me to swing my leg over him to become mounted firmly on his back. He didn't seem to be concerned about my being up there so I patted him, first on the neck, then on the rump. He watched me closely, not moving a muscle.

After I dismounted and stripped the leather off him, everything except the halter, which would make it easier to catch him later, he was free to roam the corral and to roll in the dust. As I left the corral and walked westward towards the tent, I was treated to one of the most beautiful Red Desert sunsets ever. The sun was centered almost perfectly on Spring Butte, appearing to be resting upon the butte itself. The horizon beyond the butte was almost as red as fire.

Dad was just pulling the Dutch oven out of the coals when I arrived at the tent. He had fixed a Mulligan stew, the aroma of which reminded me it had been along time since dinner. The stew was cooked to perfection. He always did make good Mulligan stew. We enjoyed it in the dusk of this tranquil evening, as we talked over the events of the day.

The sun had barely slipped down over the western horizon, when the moon began to make it's appearance from below the eastern horizon. It was an equally beautiful sight. Looking up at the full moon, my youthful mind began to explore. Were there really mountains and streams on the moon? It surely looked like there could be. Was it really all of those millions of miles from earth as the astronomers were telling us, or did they really know? It surely didn't seem possible for anyone to know.

The big dipper was easy to locate, but the little one took a little more effort. Dad had shown me how to locate the North Star in reference to the big dipper. He said "it's not true north but it is sure a good reference if you are riding in strange territory at night." After putting a couple of shovels full of dirt on the Dutch oven coals, we went inside the tent where we did the dishes and prepared to hit the hay.

Not long after we got into bed, the coyotes began to howl. Their lonely wail was almost like a lullaby, putting me to sleep. The next day I rode Seal in the corral for about a half hour, taking him out in the open when it was time to water the day herd.

As I was following the herd down the dusty desert trail, a small whirl-wind came twirling across the alkali flat, making it's way right towards me. As it struck the trail where I was riding, I was engulfed in dust and flying debris. Seal became spooked and began to run and buck. He wasn't a hard bucking horse and I soon had him under control by putting him into a spin.

Some horses have the desire and the ability to buck, born and bred right into them, others like Seal will buck if they get spooked but they don't go at it so hard.

Seal broke out real well and was sold to a dude ranch in Jackson Hole. I hated to see him go, but being so young, he was much better off on a dude ranch than in a wild horse running operation.

The Corral at Ten Mile

Dad had scouted the Ten Mile Spring area several times, looking for a good place to build a corral. He had spooked several bunches out after they had watered at the spring. Most of them would go east, up over a ridge and head for the flat. The flat lay about five miles east of the spring. It is about two miles long and one and a half miles wide. It was a very popular place for horses and a very good place for whirlwinds. You could see them nearly any time of day swirling up the alkali dust from the flat.

We picked a place in a draw about half way between the spring and the flat to build the wild horse corral. Our camp and a saddle horse corral were set up near the spring. We wouldn't have to haul our drinking water like we had to at the camp south of Black Rock. The Coal Spring was just a seepage and not fit to drink. We would winter here and trap coyotes and badgers as soon as the furs were prime. The old timers claim that any month with an R in it would mean prime furs in Wyoming.

The tent was set over a frame. We dug into the side of a hill and boarded up about three foot sides. The floor was dirt, but it packed down almost like cement. We had a good iron, wood burning stove with an oven(an old sheep camp stove), so all in all, we had a snug camp.

The winter was spent mostly trapping. It froze early and the post holes were too hard to dig for the corral, so we laid that aside until spring. We did pretty well trapping. The snow got pretty deep and I guess coyotes and badgers got hungry enough to take the bait.

This trapping was a whole new ball game for me, but I was enthusiastic about learning all I could about it. Dad was a good teacher and showed me how to boil the traps to remove human scent by putting a few handfuls of sage leaves (off the brush) in the water. Next, we cut squares of canvas about six inches

123

square and cut a slit in one side. One of these was for each trap that we had. It took a full day to get everything ready to start our trap line.

The next morning after we and the horses had been fed, we saddled up two to ride and put a pack saddle on one to carry the traps, stakes and all the other trapping equipment. Then we headed south from camp down the Ten Mile Canyon.

It had snowed about an inch during the night, but the sun was shining in the morning and everything looked clean and bright. Dad kept watching the ground. I knew he was looking for coyote and badger tracks. We hadn't gone far when he dismounted and knelt down by a fresh set of tracks. I got off my horse and got near enough to see them, too. He said they are badger tracks made in the night while it was still snowing.

I asked if we were going to set a trap here, but he said we would look for a hill or knoll to set it on so the snow would keep blown off and wouldn't cover our traps too deep. We mounted and rode on until we came to just such a knoll. Dad went to a place where the ground was bare and started digging a small hole using the sharp end of a trap stake. He didn't dig a deep hole, just a shallow one, the size to fit a trap into. Next, he set a double spring coyote trap and fitted it into the hole. At this time, I found out what the canvas was for. It was fitted over the plate and dirt was sprinkled over the whole trap until all you could see was dirt. The canvas keeps dirt from under the plate so when it was stepped on by a coyote or badger or whatever, the plate would go down and allow the trap to spring on its leg. After the trap was staked down good and part of a rabbit left for bait, we rode on looking for more places for good sets.

We rode to the southwest towards the ridge between nine mile and ten mile and made several more sets before we got to the ridge. We picked the nine mile side to eat our lunch. This was the sunny side and out of the chilly breeze that was coming from the northeast. Dad had brought the makings for coffee so he started a small fire and was brewing a pot while I just looked around a ledge of rocks near by.

There was a set of tracks there that didn't look like the badger tracks or the dog-like tracks that coyotes make. Whatever made these tracks had real round feet and only about half the size of coyotes. I called Dad over for a look. He said they were bobcat tracks. Probably a loner moving through because there wasn't enough rough rocks and cover for them to stay in there.

After we had eaten, we climbed to the highest part of the ridge and glassed the whole country. We could see seven or eight bunches of horses; most of them were east and south of ten mile. We also saw a couple of big flocks of antelope, two to three hundred each, bunched up for the winter.

We set a few traps along the rim of nine mile canyon. Then we traveled back on the ten mile rim ending up just above our camp, as it was getting dark. The wind had gradually increased and by the time we got to camp, it had started to snow.

I unsaddled the horses, fed them oats and hobbled two of them. Dad had gone directly into the tent and started a fire in the stove. By the time I got inside, the coffee was boiling and supper was on the stove. The aroma of food cooking was a real treat after being out all day on that chilly raw day.

After supper, we sat and talked for awhile. The wind made the tent shake and flutter. The kerosene lamp nearly went out a couple of times. Dad looked out and remarked about the storm. Finally we turned in. It was kind of an eerie feeling sleeping out in our tent, knowing that we were the only human beings in at least twenty miles.

I woke up early the next morning to the sound of the northwest wind blowing snow against the tent. Dad opened the flap and looked out, then remarked that it must have snowed and blown all night. He soon had the coffee pot boiling on the stove as the fire under the lids snapped and cracked. Dad used to say "let it storm, we were here first."

It was a good feeling to know that we had plenty of wood piled up to last out quite a storm. We were running pretty short of grub, however. My brother Don, who usually brought groceries on weekends, had to work the Saturday night shift in the coal mine at Superior and hadn't made his usual trip to restock our supplies. Dad was about out of Bull Durham smoking to-bacco, too.

This seemed pretty critical to him.

We didn't attempt to leave the camp that day. We just ven-tured outside to take care of our personal chores and feed the dogs. The saddle horses would be down in the washout, above camp, out of the storm. Dad had gotten some heavy leather in town to rebuild the rigging in my old saddle so I could rope from it. We got busy doing this and took advantage of the stormy day.

We dismantled the old cogshell saddle, took out the old rig-ging and put in the new, including a back cinch. We also made two pair of hobbles, using heavy leather, buckles and copper rivets. One pair was side hobbles. This pair had about a 2 foot length of chain between the leather cuffs. Side hobbles go on a front and a rear ankle. They are used on horses that get too good at running with their two front feet together when they are regularly hobbled.

It got dark early again without any sign of sun or blue sky. It seemed to be getting colder. Dad remarked that it would probably clear off in the night. We had a few potatoes left so we put the sack between the bed blankets so they wouldn't freeze. I woke up a couple of times in the night and the wind was still blowing snow against the tent.

It was still snowing lightly and the wind was moving it right on across country in the morning when we got up. The plan was that I would leave for Superior as soon as the storm quit, if it was before noon. It would take a good half day to ride to Su-perior.

The weather continued to improve and about mid-morning the saddle horses came into camp looking for their grain. We fed them and began preparing for my journey. I saddled up Tippy, a seal brown horse with a white tip on his nose. He was one of my favorites. We put the pack saddle on a little bay mare we called Lady. She was gentle, would pack anything and led real well. I should make it to Superior by sundown where I'd spend the night with my brothers and sisters and return to camp the next day. This would be a treat for me because my oldest sister, Marcy, would be there with her baby, Don Kopp. We had already nick-named him Pete.

I got lonesome for the rest of the family at times, but mostly we stayed busy at camp and I really enjoyed that.

The brown took off at a brisk trot and we headed west. There was still a little breeze, enough to make my cheeks red, but it wasn't real cold. I was taking the shortest way to Superior. There wasn't any trail this way but it was much closer than to follow the trail.

The Nine Mile Rim didn't seem as high as usual and I was soon over it and into Nine Mile Canyon. Following a long narrow ridge to the mouth of this canyon brought me out into the canyon that now has the "Jim Bridger Generating Plant" in it.

The washout in the bottom was deep and it took awhile to find a place where I could cross. Traveling northwest, it wasn't much out of my way. Once across the wash, I headed again up a deep draw that leads up to the top of the big ridge of lava rock hills just east of town. The sun was just setting as I neared the top. The snow was getting deeper as I gained elevation. The wind hadn't been blowing down in the canyons and draws, but I could see the snow sifting over the ridges now, and as the sun went down it got gradually colder.

By the time I got out on the top the snow was belly deep to the horses and crusted hard on top. I dismounted and led the horses. I could walk on top of the snow crust, but the horses broke through and really made traveling difficult for them. The distance across the flat top is probably three miles, but it seemed like ten this night. It was dark by the time I got halfway across. Luckily, there was a full moon, so I could see real well. The wind kept blowing the snow and it felt like it was cutting my face. The horses were getting tired and my toes and fingers didn't have any feeling left. By the time we reached the west rim and looked down upon Superior, we were all perked up by the sight of lights and smoke that seemed to hang over the town in a cloud.

We took the steep road leading down into Superior. I walked about a half mile, then mounted up and took the last mile and a half at a trot. The odor of coal smoke smelled good to me.

After the horses were put away in Enor Makkis' corral and fed, I walked to the house for the reunion with the rest of the family. There was a good fire in the old kitchen range, and a big pot of chili simmering on the back.

This really hit the spot and I was soon warmed and visiting. However, I didn't get to bounce Pete on my knee until the next morning. His mother had put him to bed and he was sleeping soundly. Sweed and Jean filled me in on what they had been doing in school. Don was working the swing shift at the mine and wouldn't be home until after midnight. I didn't last that long because with a full belly and a warmed body I soon got the drowsies and crawled into bed.

Awakened the next morning by the slamming of the back door, I decided it was time to get up and look alive. The kids had just left for school, which accounted for the slammed door. Don soon got up and fixed a batch of sour dough pancakes. He really had a way with that sour dough, making bread and buns with it, too. Marcy, Don and I sat around the table and I told them about how many traps we had set and about the storm. We soon began rounding up supplies for my pack, as I wanted to start back as early as possible. I got mostly staple foods, kerosene for the lamp, and ended up with a carton of Bull Durham for Dad.

The morning was half gone when I rode out of Superior. The sun was bright and no sign of a breeze. It was a beautiful morning. the trip back to camp was quite uneventful. I walked and led Tippy back across the top where the snow was so deep, and took the same way back as I had come the night before.

Back at the horse camp, Dad was patiently waiting for me. His tobacco supply completely exhausted, he had even mixed the last with used coffee grounds dried out on the back of the stove. this was an old tobacco stretching trick that he learned from Bill Lewis.

It wasn't until the next morning at breakfast that we discovered the kerosene had been packed too close to the oatmeal and had leaked just enough to make it taste real bad of kerosene. We had to dump it out after packing it all that distance.

Just after breakfast we saddled up a couple of horses, called the hounds and started out to run our north trap line. It was another bright, sunny day and we rode up over the rim towards twelve mile. We hadn't gone far when we spotted fresh coyote tracks. We tracked him for about a mile. Tracking was easy in the new snow and the brush was pretty well covered on the flat. The tracks eventually led to the head of a little draw where the brush was taller and could easily hide a coyote.

We decided to split up. I'd go down and approach it from the downhill side. Dad would keep the dogs and stay above, hoping the coyote would run out on the flat, giving the dogs a better chance to catch him.

I got about half-way to the draw when the coyote ran out of the brush and was headed full speed down the ridge across the draw from me. I put the spurs to my horse thinking I might head him off. My chase ended abruptly when my horse hit the draw full of snow which was deeper than I thought. He upset and I bit the snow but landed clear, so I didn't get rolled on. By the time I was up, Dad came riding up to see if I was hurt.

The dogs had seen the coyote and took after him. After I had assured Dad that I was okay, he followed the chase. They were a long ways from me, but I watched as they gained distance on him. they were just about to go over a ridge when I saw Queenie flip him. She was the fastest and also the smallest of the hounds. Running at full speed she would put her nose between a coyote's hind legs and flip him. This caused the coyote to lose his footing and roll. By the time he regained his footing and before he could get going the other two would be there for the kill.

By this time, I had shook most of the snow off and, except for being wet down my front where the snow went down my open collar, I was okay and ready to go again. My horse had stayed close to me and was picking away at a few spears of grass that stuck out above the snow. I caught him and walked on up the ridge where I met Dad. The coyote that we had caught was a big dog and had beautiful light colored fur. Dad figured he'd bring eight to ten dollars.

We continued on around the trap line. We hadn't caught any in the traps yet and I was getting a little impatient. Dad explained that usually you can't expect to catch anything the first few days after you set traps because there is always human scent. Coyotes are smart animals and stay away from anything that would appear unusual to them, like freshly dug dirt and the smell of humans. One of our traps had a badger in it so we had a pretty good day after all.

Back in camp we skinned our catch and put the skins on stretchers to dry. The rest of the winter went pretty fast. We rode the trap line every other day and seemed to catch our share of coyotes and badgers.

As soon as spring came, we went back to building our corral. Don had gathered some used railroad ties for posts. They worked good, and were solid once we got them set and tamped into the ground. We also had some pine posts that had been used as stakes on flat rail cars used to haul mine timbers.

The main corral was #9 woven wire reinforced with about five cables stretched very tightly around the outside and fastened with stay wires. the posts were about four feet apart. The wings were mostly two cables out towards the end and four up closer to the corral. Out at the end of the wings the posts were camouflaged with sage brush so the horses wouldn't see them until they were quite close to the corral. By this time they would be busting over a little ridge and right into the trap.

We worked hard at building the corral and talked about catching some of the big bunches of mustangs that we had seen to the east of Ten Mile. We had hoped to get a chance at that half & half that I had seen over by coal Spring. Those two times were all that we had seen him.

There was a buckskin stud with four stocking legs up to his knees and a bald face that we had seen several times. He ran with three other young studs that had been kicked out of herds by older studs. These young stallions were a bunch of movers. They could run fast and keep it up all day. We always planned to relay the buckskin and tire him out until we could rope him. We could probably rope him off water, but it seems to ruin them to rope them with a belly full of water. They don't seem to have as much zip after that.

The day finally came when we could try our new corral. We picked a weekend so Don, Sweed and Jean could be out there to help us. We got a good early start that Saturday morning. After a short huddle to decide who would be where, including a little plan drawn in the dirt with a stick, we saddled up. Sweed rode Lady, Don had Appy, a long-legged bay that had to crow hop a little and warm you up every morning, and I rode Tippy. Dad and Jean, riding Shorty and Pappy, would move the day herd out on the ridge towards the corral and wait and watch. If we got fairly close with a wild bunch, they would move the gentler horses into the wings of the corral. They worked as decoys.

We followed a horse trail to the north, up out of Ten Mile Canyon. Reaching the top of the ridge we stopped and glassed the countryside to the east. We spotted several bunches east of the flat. the closest herd was about five miles away. We couldn't decide which one we wanted until we got closer. We left Sweed on the ridge in a place where he could get out of sight but could still see. He would turn them off on the lower ridge towards the corral. Don and I rode on to the east.

We singled out a bunch of ten head that was quite a ways from any other bunch. We figured we could get around them without spooking them. Don went clear around east of them and I stopped northwest of them about a quarter of a mile away. I stepped off my horse, checked the cinch and patted Tippy on the neck. His ears were pointed ahead and he was watching. We seemed to be assuring each other that we were ready for the chase. I had that same nervous, excited feeling that I always got before starting a herd.

Don was out of sight from me for awhile, but when I saw him next he was just over a little knoll behind the wild bunch. He was leading his horse so he could stay low and not be seen until he was close to them. He mounted up and barreled straight towards the bunch. They wasted no time getting started and they headed west. They were soon even with me and I was mounted and ready. When the lead mare saw me she really got into high gear and tried to go north. I gave Tippy his head and he could run pretty good but that old mare was no slouch either. We were neck and neck for about two miles. The bunch was strung out quite far but Don was bringing up the rear. I soon found myself entangled in a bunch of short draws and taller brush. I would have to ride wide on them and hope the old mare would slack off and let the rest catch up.

By pulling away to the side, I had to give some ground, but, by the same token, the old lead mare slowed a little with the pressure off her. By this time things weren't looking so good, they had gotten too far north to be turned in time for Sweed to push them down the ridge. I kept on at a good clip, finally getting on good going again and was able to gain on them. The old stud took the lead at this point and I felt that they were going to make it into Twelve Mile Canyon, when all of a sudden they turned sharply back southwest. This direction was little more to my liking.

As I rode along at a pretty fast gait, I went over a little ridge and darned near ran through a band of sheep. This is what had turned the wild ones. The sheepherder sat on a little knoll close by holding the reins of his horse. I waved to him. He waved back and I continued on my way.

The bunch headed right for the rim that separates Ten Mile from Nine Mile Canyon. I didn't think they would go into Nine Mile but would try to go towards Black Rock. There was a smooth looking little ridge that I headed for. I was giving Tippy a little breather because that old stud was sure to challenge me when I tried to turn them.

When it became apparent to the stud that I was between him and where he wanted to go, he really poured the coal on. This time he had the disadvantage, he was in rougher going than I was. Soon he turned and the whole bunch went full speed down into Ten Mile. This was working out real well. Not as we had planned it originally, but in our favor anyway. Things seldom go as planned when running wild horses. Those old ponies have minds of their own and you just have to work them the best way you can. Everybody involved has to be alert at all times to see what is going on so they can be in the right place at the right time.

Sweed had remained out of sight of the bunch the whole time but he was where he could see the horses. Now he rode down into Ten Mile Canyon where he would wait until the wild ones passed him. He would show up behind them and push them up the hill at top speed. Don had cut across to be near the corral so he could help corral them if they came that way.

Dad had been where he couldn't see any of the action until Sweed came riding down into Ten Mile. He knew then that we had a bunch headed his way. Dad and Jean got the day herd set in the wings and got off to the side and got off their horses, remaining on the opposite side of the mounts from which the herd would appear.

The wild ones were pretty tired by the time they reached the top of the ridge east of Ten Mile. They spotted our day herd and made right for it. Just abut the time they got to the day herd, Dad, Jean, Don and Sweed were all right behind them yelling like a bunch of Comanche's. They hustled right on over the hill and into our corral. We had really christened it right with the first bunch we tried.

I hadn't kept up with the pace of the wild ones after they went into Ten Mile. Tippy was breathing pretty hard, so I took it slow. Being close enough to see the dust as they burst over the hill towards the corral was a big thrill for me. I rode up just as they had the gate securely tied. Dad rolled a smoke and handed the makings to Don. This is the way they always ended an exciting chase.

We pulled the saddles off the three tired saddle horses and began walking them to cool them down. We would sponge off their backs with cool water and rub their legs with absorbine when we got back to camp.

The day herd would remain in the corral with the wild ones all night. This would help to tame them down so they wouldn't run into the side of the corral trying to get out. We didn't bother them anymore that day except for a quick look to see what we had.

They were all dark-colored horses. The stud was brown. There were three spring colts and two yearlings. One mare was branded with a brand that we couldn't make out.

By the time we got back to camp, the horses were pretty well cooled down. We stopped at the spring and gave them only about four swallows of water each. After supper we would give them grain and turn them loose. They could drink more then without hurting them.

We sat around in the tent after our meal of mulligan stew. Dad had put it into the Dutch oven in a bed of hot coals and covered it with more hot coals and then dirt over the top to seal it up. He had done this in the morning before he left. It was an excellent supper for a tired and hungry bunch of wild horse runners. We relived the whole day of excitement, each telling his part, and highlights of the chase. Soon after we had gone to bed the coyotes began to howl. Dad remarked that we hadn't caught all of them. This was music to my ears and I was soon sound asleep.

We were up early the next morning. By the time I got the saddle horses wrangled, Dad had bacon frying. the odor came out through the open tent flap and all of a sudden I was really hungry. After we finished breakfast, we saddled up and rode back to the corral. This was the day for branding.

The wild ones had settled down pretty well over night. The first thing we did was turn the branded mare out with her colt. They took off at a brisk trot for a little ways then realized that part of their bunch was still in the corral. They called back and forth to each other for a little while, then they disappeared over a hill.

Dad roped the stud first, catching him around the neck. Next, he took a couple of wraps around the snubbing post in the round corral. This old horse had never had anything like this happen to him before. He felt the rope tighten on his neck and he reared up and gave a big squeal, pawing the air with his front feet. then he began pulling back on the rope. The harder he pulled, the tighter the noose pulled around his neck. He soon ran out of air and dropped to the ground. In an instant, Don was on his head holding it in a way that would make it hard for the horse to get up. At the same time, he loosened the noose and the stud breathed easily again. By this time, Dad had a loop on his front feet and tied them with one hind foot pulled up between them. He wasn't able to get up tied like this. Dad mouthed him and said his teeth showed him to be twelve or fourteen years old. He would probably go to the mink farm because he was too old to break for a saddle horse. We put our $\overline{c}_{\overline{\mathcal{J}}}$ brand on his right thigh, trimmed his tail and let him up.

The rest of the branding went very much like this. The younger ones didn't fight as much and didn't choke down. They were roped by the front feet and upset by getting behind them and pulling their feet out from under them. We tied the yearlings up with a heavy rope around their flank, up between their front legs and through the halter ring. They would pull on this for a couple of days and soon would lead. These young wild horses gentled down and broke real easy when they found out that we wouldn't hurt them. We would start feeding them a few oats right away. They really went for that.

We weren't always as lucky at corralling the wild ones as we were on that first bunch. Sometimes we would end up with two or three, sometimes none. We did catch a few good bunches though.

One bunch we had run for a long ways. We had about run our saddle horses all down by the time we got them to the wings of the corral. We couldn't get them turned in and knew we wouldn't be able to bring them back.

Don was riding a sorrel horse that we had gotten out of Utah. He roped a big bay mare and the little sorrel turned wrong and it pulled him off his feet. It also broke the cinch and Don went for a ride hanging onto the saddle with the wild mare dragging him. The saddle soon drug hard enough in the brush to stop her and Dad got a rope on her.

In the meantime, I had run upon a small yearling. I didn't have a rope, so I took hold of his mane and jumped off and bull dogged him. He never did go down but came to a stop until Sweed came with a short rope from the corral. This was when we decided I'd have to carry a rope.

I had broken Tippy the year before and had been riding Slicker some this spring. They were brothers out of the L Stud. They were marked alike but Tippy was seal brown and Slicker, a bright bay. Tippy was four now and Slicker only three years old. We didn't use them for running very much until they were four or five years old. Tippy never did buck with me but Slicker was something else. Once in awhile he would take to me and buck, but usually he could be talked out of it.

One day, Dad rode him on the trap line and all of a sudden he started to buck and soon lost Dad, who was not looking to be treated this way. the horse let him catch him again and mount up and continue the trap line without any more monkey business. We figured one of the hounds probably was following behind in the trail and bumped his heels with it's nose to Trigger such a performance. Whatever the cause, he didn't gain any popularity points in camp and I had him pretty much to myself from then on.

One weekend we had run a bunch on Saturday, but had lost them. We decided to try the same bunch on Sunday, if we could locate them. We didn't have very many fresh saddle horses since we had used several of them the day before. We would never use them hard two days in a row. This Sunday I rode Slicker and would stay with the day herd. Don and Sweed went down on the long run and Dad went about half way down.

They couldn't find the same bunch that we had run on Saturday. They looked for a long time, but finally settled for a different bunch. They ran them a good long ways and finally got them turned down into Ten Mile. They were coming about right for a long time but after crossing the draw below the spring they went south. They came up a ridge about a half mile south of the corral.

When the wild bunch topped the ridge, I was mounted up and waiting. I was hoping I could turn them up the ridge towards the waiting day herd and the corral. The leader at this point was a buckskin mare. As soon as she saw me she was off and running in spite of her tiredness. The ridge gradually sloped downward to the east for about one half mile then got steeper and ended up on Ten Mile Flat. Slicker was ready to run as usual and didn't have any trouble out-running that lead mare. The main bunch had strung out quite a long ways and the tail end began to cut across behind me. The leaders that I had partially turned soon stopped and cut behind me to join the rest of the herd. By this time, I had decided that I wouldn't get the bunch turned back without making another big swing with them. This is what I had sworn against, because to do so might ruin my young saddle horse.

Everyone else had tired horses so I decided to try to salvage something out of a hard day's running. In less time that it takes to tell, I decided to try to rope one. Still riding at a run, I was unbuckling the strap that held my lariat to the saddle. The rope was tied hard and fast to the saddle, the only way to rope horses. Wild horses are too fast to try to dally and you only lose a good rope. To tie hard and fast we ran the end of the rope from the front through the hole in the pommel of the saddle and took two half hitches around the horn.

There had been a little Grulla (smokey buckskin) stud running right behind the lead mare. This is the one I decided on. Searching him out, I put Slicker on his tail and built a good sized loop. Slicker soon ate up the distance that separated me from a prize catch. The wild stallion was really pouring on the coal by this time. The dust was thick and small particles of dirt and small stones hit my face. By squinting my eyes, I was able to see. I knew we were getting close to the steep down hill grade and I would only get one chance to rope the buckskin stud. I swung the loop around above my head once, twice, then let drive with all of my strength. The noose settled nicely over the wild one's head. This had to be my lucky day because I hadn't done that much roping and was by no means an expert.

The stud put on an extra burst of speed, and as he hit the end of the rope, I was loosened up in the saddle. My feet were out of the stirrups expecting Slicker to be pulled off his feet because he had never been used for roping before. Instead, he faltered once, but soon regained his footing and we began slowing the pace to a gradual stop. The stud hit the end of the rope several times, squealed and pawed the air but the manila rope held as did everything else. This was the first time I had tried out my saddle for roping since we rebuilt the rigging.

Dad and Sweed soon came riding up and put another rope on the wild one. With one holding from each side and Sweed directly behind, we hazed him to the corral where he was tied up to be halter broke.

Later that night, as we sat around the campfire, I told the rest that I was sorry I had lost the bunch. Dad said he figured they knew where the corral was and would never go into it. At least we had one nice, two year old, smoky buckskin stud to show for a hard days work for horses and riders.

As the summer progressed, we tried several more bunches. All of them had apparently found the corral as they went to the spring to water. the decision to move the corral to Twelve Mile was made after one of the unsuccessful runs had been made. At Twelve Mile we picked a place about a half mile below the spring, fairly close to the wash. It was farther from any well used trails than the corral at Ten Mile had been.

Don had bought an old Dodge car that had been cut off and had a box on the back. This was the truck that we used to move everything from Ten Mile to Twelve Mile. This was the first vehicle that I ever got to drive alone. It was about a '1926' model. There was no fuel pump but it had a vacuum tank that supplied the gas to the carburetor. One trip Sweed and I had taken a load over by ourselves and ran out of gas right in the bottom of the draw in Twelve Mile. We had to walk back to Ten Mile. Boy!, we were dragging our ends by the time we got back.

During this time, WWII had gotten bad and my two older brothers, Chuck and Don had entered the Army. This didn't leave us much help so the corral building went slow.

We were about halfway done with our corral when Frank Robbins pulled into camp with a Model A ford truck loaded with posts and wire, etc. He was headed for a place called Chalk buttes to build a big corral to use in rounding up wild horses with a plane. He had been hit by the war, too and couldn't get help. He wanted us to go in with him and build his corral. We would take our day herd and use them like we had been doing. He didn't keep a day herd but seemed to like the way ours worked as decoys.

Frank explained how the lay of the land was; how the wings of the corral would come up behind two knolls. Everything was completely hidden. The horses would be well down into the wings before they would see any posts or anything. This seemed like a good set-up to us. We agreed to go down and help him although we were about tired of building corrals by this time.

Two days later we were putting a pack on Lady and getting ready for a trek across the "Red Strip" to chalk Buttes. We took our small tent, a bed roll, clothing and a few other necessities. We didn't have to take food and utensils because Mrs. Robbins was out there and we would eat with them.

We had a good sized day herd built up. Some of the last ones caught were still plenty spooky and spook they did when they saw the horse with the pack on its back. We got out of there at a lively clip, luckily they got started the right direction. Dad got around them just before they crossed Black rock Wash. I was leading the pack mare and was considerably slower. By the time I arrived on the scene, they had settled down pretty well and we turned the pack mare loose with the herd. We grazed them for a good hour in the nice green grass that was in the low land around Black Rock Wash.

It was nearly sundown by the time we reached the Red Strip. This was the first time I had been to the Strip. The ground is very red in color. The soil is different from anything I have ever seen. It is crumbly and soft. Horses sink into it to their ankles. This tires a saddle horse real fast. Luckily, it is only about a mile or mile and a half wide. From the strip it wasn't far to Chalk Buttes. We were there just at sundown. It was easy to see why they had been named Chalk Buttes. they showed up white as the sun was setting on them. They rose about 200 feet above the desert floor.

Frank had made a holding corral for the day herd which we put them into after they watered at the dug-out. Dad and Frank went about setting our tent up while I cared for the saddle horses. By the time we finished, it was dark and Mrs. Robbins had supper ready. We washed up outside the camp wagon and went inside to meet Mrs. Robbins. She appeared to be a very pleasant lady; seemed quiet to me. She had prepared a meal fit for a king which we thoroughly enjoyed. The pie she baked reminded me of home, but we hadn't seen much pie since the passing of mother.

After supper, we sat in the camp of "Wild Horse Robbins" and visited. He told us of the plan to build the corral and of his many experiences running horses. He told us of seeing a horse that was one half white and half dark colored, and if we got that one, it would belong to his wife. We told him that we had seen it too, but didn't make a fuss about giving it to Mrs. Robbins; we'd have to catch him first. It must have been midnight when we turned in. Anyway, it was a short night.

We had the day herd out to graze before sun up. They hadn't had much to eat the day before with the traveling so we gave them a good fill. To the northwest of the buttes the land lay fairly level and open for a couple of miles. The soil was sandy and wild rice grass grows in bunches in this type of soil. Horses really like it and do well on it. The seed is just like grain. Most of the time we would just let the day herd graze in the daytime, checking on them once in a while to see that they didn't stray.

When the corral was about half done, I expressed my concern that I hadn't seen many bunches of wild horses around Chalk Buttes. Frank said this didn't matter, they could bring them a long ways with the plane. There were a lot of horses to the northwest on Buffalo Hump and the Buffalo Bench. There were many bunches on the Red Strip farther east, too. There were always horses along the sand hills to the west.

The corral was nearly done and the date had been set for Everette Hogan to fly in. These were exciting times for me. there was a chance that I would get my first plane ride. The corral looked especially good too and we felt that it couldn't miss.

The morning the plane arrived, Frank and I were both out with the day herd. The plane looked like a big eagle from where we were. It circled the camp a couple of times. Frank rode into camp right away and I brought the horses in.

Hogan had landed the Piper Cub on a salt sage flat near the water dugout. By the time I got the horses in the corral they were fueling the plane with gas that Frank had brought from town. Hogan had flown from his home in Scotts Bluff, Nebraska and would take no chances of running out of gas while running mustangs on the Red Desert.

Robbins Roundup

The first run to be made with the plane was to produce the Half & Half horse. Frank rode with the pilot so they would be more sure of locating the bunch. Deep down I hoped they wouldn't find him. That was one horse I would really like to have in our own string of saddle horses.

Dad and I had taken the day herd out to graze a short distance north and straight out from the corral wings. There was a light breeze blowing from the north. This was in our favor. The wild ones wouldn't get our scent until they were well down into the wings of the corral. We watched from one of the highest of the Chalk Buttes. The plane was criss-crossing the desert floor. First, crossing the sand hills, then back across to Twelve Mile Rim and back past Black Rock. They could sure cover a lot of ground in a hurry with that Piper Cub. They were out of our hearing range, but we could see the plane as the pilot would bank around and almost dive down towards the ground for a better look at a wild herd of mustangs.

This went on for about two hours and finally the plane headed back east towards the Chalk Buttes. Now the plane was making tight banking turns and operating close to the ground. We could see the desert dust begin to boil up and we knew they had a big bunch headed our way. Soon we could hear the plane's engine and we began to work the day herd into the wings of the corral. We didn't have long to wait after we had positioned the day herd and had each gotten behind the little knoll at the end of the wings.

The first horse to come into sight was the Half & Half. That wild stallion was stretched out and really running, trying to lead his harem safely away from that big mechanical bird that was always swooping down upon them. The rest of the horses were strung out for about a mile; most of them engulfed in a cloud of dust. We couldn't even guess how many there might be. The stud would try to circle back towards Twelve Mile

The rest of the horses were strung out for about a mile.

where his home range was. The Chalk Butte Corral was built on a natural get-away for wild horses. Once they were on the red strip it was almost impossible to overtake them on a saddle horse. The softness of the strip made it real hard for a horse to run fast carrying a rider. When the tail-end of the wild bunch finally entered the wings, Dad and I rode out yelling at the top of our voices to flush them into the corral and to keep the first ones from coming back out.

As I rode up over the last little hill overlooking the corral, I had a very happy moment. Out into the red strip were about ten head of horses running for dear life. They were being led by a beautiful stallion who was half white and half dark. He reminded me of a wild buck antelope, as he ran very fast trying to maintain his freedom.

We ended up with about twenty head of wild ones in the corral. The Half & Half and the other ones that got away run through the wing of the corral at the bottom of the hill.

The next day, Dad rode with Hogan in the plane. I believe that was Dad's only plane ride. He thoroughly enjoyed it. The most fun of all was being able to pass up any stud on the desert. The wind blew hard the following day and I didn't get to ride in the plane. We corralled many large herds of mustangs in the three days that we used the plane.

The branding was a big job that lasted two days. The older mares and stallions that acted like they would give us trouble in the day herd, were given special treatment. They got their nostrils sewn shut with one strand of buckskin. They weren't tight enough to shut off breathing, but restricted it when they ran. They couldn't run far until they were out of breath. This was a new method of handling wild ones to us, but Frank had used it for a long time. This seemed like quite an inhumane treatment until I saw it done. They just made a small incision in the outer edge of each nostril and put the thick buckskin string through and drew it part way shut. We had always side-hobbled the trouble makers or tied up a front foot. They didn't go far that way either. We had so many to do and sewing was no doubt the quickest and easiest way to handle them. They would take off and run for about a quarter of a mile, they were easy to bring back to the day herd. After about three or four times like that we could easily clip the buckskin, and they would be just like the rest of the bunch. The first couple of days we kept them in the spacious wings of the corral. We hadn't let the day herd graze in there and the grass was good to begin with, but after two days the horses were glad to get out in the open.

We began trailing the herd eastward to eventually end our trail drive in Rawlins. We were to put on a wild horse rodeo in the fair grounds there. The advertising was already up. Frank had taken care of this during one of his trips to town. He had also brought Dave Alley out on one of his trips.

Dave was about my age, and had helped Frank the summer before, so he was a good hand with horses. I liked him right from the start and enjoyed having someone my age to talk to. We spent the first night out from the Chalk Buttes at the Red Desert Ranch. We slept in the bunk house there.

This part of the desert was all strange to me but it was nice to see a ranch out in the middle of nowhere. They had a dam

Mustang mare—probably about 30 years old. Corraled by airplane by Robbins.

across a small draw and irrigated a little land so it really showed up green on the desert.

Up at daybreak and breakfast under our belts, we soon had the herd out to graze. After a couple of hours in a deep grass covered draw, the horses were ready to continue on the way. The road we followed leading eastward from the Red Desert Ranch was nothing more than a trail. There were two tracks winding their way through the sage brush and around deep washouts. Frank led the way with his Model A Ford truck. He had a precious cargo consisting of a big grub box, inside of which was all the food we would need for the trip, our bed rolls, and grain for our saddle horses.

The old truck bounced along at a slow pace. We could nearly keep up to it with the horses. About mid-day, we rode up
over a little hill and Frank was there with lunch fixed for us.
He had stopped by a dug out cabin that he had built a few years
earlier. It was dug into the side of a hill and the front was made
of old rail-road ties. It had one window, one door and a dirt
floor.

There was a good spring of water so we all had a cold drink
and watered the herd. The grass was good around the spring so
the horses filled up real good.

Our stop for the night was at an artesian well where Frank
had a water trap built. We camped quite a ways back from the
well because there was fresh sign around and we knew horses
were watering there. I had heard about water traps, but this
was the first one I had ever seen. The whole thing was a heavy
duty corral, made of heavy gauge woven wire and cables. The
heavy posts were close together just like a regular wild horse
corral. The whole thing was built in a circular shape completely enclosing the well, and all of the water in a pond made by
the continuous flowing of the well. This was the only water
hole for miles in this old Red Desert and the horses were almost forced into drinking there.

The sun was sinking in the west as we neared the flowing-
well horse trap. There hadn't been many wild bunches in sight
all day along the trail and I was a little disappointed at the
thought of not having a chance to use the trap. We would be
leaving early the next morning and I would sure like to see it
work.

Frank had baked baking powder biscuits in the Dutch oven
and had a kettle of cowboy beans for supper. The chow was really good after a hard day in the saddle. After the dishes were
done and everything put away, Frank took his station by the
gate of the water trap. He said the horses came from a long
ways off to water here and not to be surprised if we got a
bunch in the night.

The rest of us turned in early. I laid there awake for quite
awhile, looking up at a sky full of Milky Way. In the distance a
bitch coyote and her pups were talking things over. I figured

they would like to get a drink at the well, but would be afraid, with us so near. Sleep finally overtook me, but about midnight, Dad shook me and said "listen." I could hear horses trotting. They were getting closer, then they stopped. There was a lot of snorting and circling of the whole area. They were being real cautious and I was just sure they would run away anytime. Finally, they became real quiet and just walked through the opening to get their much-needed drink of water. Frank slammed the hinged gate on them and that was when all hell broke loose. They began hitting the sides of the corral and the sparks really flew as the cables and wire were forced together. We heard a few horses run away into the night, but had no way of knowing how many leaked out.

We stayed away from the trap because our presence would only make them more afraid. Frank came up and crawled into his bed. He said he figured there were about ten or twelve that came in, but didn't know how many had gotten away.

Dad had slipped quietly out of bed without waking me up. The sun was just peeking over the horizon displaying all the beauty of a Red Desert sunrise. The sound that I awoke to was "come and get it." Dave Alley had slept in too. We wouldn't be able to get the herd out to graze before the wild ones that we trapped in the night were branded. Just after breakfast, Dave and I worked our way slowly and quietly down to the trap for a quick look at what we had caught. There was a sorrel stud, one sorrel mare and two bay mares. Each mare had a sorrel colt. That stud really caught my eye. He wasn't much taller than old Pappy but was a real fine-boned horse. This slim and sleek horse, with his shiny coat, looked like he would really be fast. His tail and mane were quite long so we knew he wasn't a very young horse.

Later in the day I told Dad that I would like to have the stud. He said he had mouthed him when he was down to be branded and his teeth showed him to be ten or eleven years old. This was too old to be practical to break him so I gave that idea up.

This day took us past the Chain Lakes. There are several small lakes connected together that make up the chain. We saw many bunches of horses near them. There are some real good horses in the area. They are mixed buckskin and roan. In the winter they get buckskin hair and shed off to be roan in the spring. They still have the dorsal stripe down the back and the jackass markings behind the knees and over the shoulders. Frank had a couple of saddle horses in his string that were Chain Lakers. They were fast and really tough horses. Chain Lake horses are from Texas blood. About mid-afternoon a cloud bank began showing up in the northwest. October had arrived and we were reminded that it was fall.

We arrived at the abandoned stage station, which is about twenty miles north of Rawlins, about an hour before dark. It was misting a little and we were glad for the shelter of the old hotel. There was an old heating stove inside, and we soon had a fire going to take the chill off. Dave and I had a look around the old hotel. There weren't over six or eight rooms. This must have been quite a place in it's day. It was a relay station where they changed horses on the stages. The good spring of water out back was no doubt the main reason for its being built there. This was an oasis in the desert country.

As we sat around the crackling stove in the abandoned stage station, we reminisced about the day's happenings. The Chain Lakes area was of special interest to me. We had passed it rather quickly, without taking the time to look the area over. It was an area alive with wild horses of a strain not common to the rest of the desert. Frank told us about these outstanding horses. His favorite horse, Old Buck, was a Chain Laker, as well as Parkoon and Chipmunk. These horses were roans, standing up well on long legs. Old Buck showed buckskin breeding, having the dorsal stripe and the jackass stripes behind the knees. In winter his coat was buckskin color, while in summer after he had shed, his color was roan. Robbins said when he was in the Cavalry breaking horses for the army, he saw many horses shipped in to be broken. Horses just like the Chain Lakers came from Texas. They were called Copper Bottom strain. They broke out well and were good horses like the Chain Lakers were. He said he felt certain the horses were of the same breeding. The original stock probably being of Spanish origin. The horses at the Chain Lakes weren't all this color and conformation but many bunches were dominated by it. At the Hanson's Desert Ranch, they had a white horse in the barn at the time we spent the night there. He was a beautiful horse with pink skin. He looked like he would qualify for the albino registry. I'm not sure there was such a thing at that time. Frank noticed my interest in the horse and told me he had come from the Chain Lakes. He said the mother was a gray mare that threw a white colt like this one every time she foaled.

He said people would go to the lakes specially to see if this mare had foaled a white colt. He said she didn't foal every year, but when she did, someone nearly always got the colt before it reached one year old. Of course this wasn't legal but when there is no one around, who would ever know who took it?"

After a good nights sleep on the floor of one of the old hotel rooms, we headed the herd south. We grazed them a lot because we didn't have far to go this last leg of our journey. Just after sundown we corralled them at a little ranch just north of Rawlins. We took them into the fair grounds the next day. Several people rode out to meet us and to help us. We needed all the help we could get. Some of the wildest ones tried to break away when the first train came whistling through.

The next day was rodeo time. This was strictly a wild horse rodeo. There was no calf roping, steer riding or bull dogging. The first event was saddle bronc riding. The only event I entered was the wild horse race. Dave and I both entered that. Mostly, we were real busy helping with the stock behind the chutes. I dropped everything and made my way to the arena when I heard the announcer say, "Mickey McKnight coming out of chute #3." Mick was one of my favorite people. He was a drifter, going from ranch to ranch. He'd work awhile, but never long at the same place. The guy was a real talented artist. He did western scenes free hand. I'm sure he could have sold pictures, but I doubt if he ever got more than a few drinks for them.

When Dad worked at Chiltons, Mick came riding in on a little bronc. He had to ride it into the corral because it wasn't broke to lead. There wasn't any brand on it and he never did say where he got it. Mick was there a few days and then left. He left the same night our buckskin and bobtailed horses disappeared. Dad saw him about six months later and jumped him about taking the horses. He said, "Heck Jake, they weren't much good anyway. I'll bring you a better pair." Like Dad said, "What do you do with a guy like that"? He had a way about him that you couldn't hate.

At the wild horse rodeo, Mick had drawn an iron gray stud that we'd had for about three months. He was really snakey. We hadn't done anything towards breaking him because he was a chunky horse and not really saddle-horse material. We had figured he would make some outfit a good pack horse. The old gray was fighting the chutes pretty bad and I was sure Mick had drawn a good horse. Mick gave his hat that final pull to snug it down on his head and said, "let him out." The chute gate flew open and out into the arena came a gray ball of fire and a very determined cowboy. The horse was determined to unseat the rider, and the rider was determined to stay aboard until the 8 second whistle sounded. The gray was a strong horse and hit the ground hard. About the third jump, the whole seat ripped out of Mick's Levis. He made a championship ride until the whistle blew and then was picked off by a pick-up man.

Back with the horses behind the chutes, we were kept busy filling the chutes with fresh horses. I kept thinking about the wild horse race. This gave me a nervous feeling and made me feel a little weak in the knees. I had experienced this many times before and it would leave as soon as the action started.

Mickey McKnight had agreed to help me in the race. I had drawn the smooth sorrel stud that we had caught in the flowing-well water trap. Each horse was let out of a chute with nothing on but a lariat rope around his neck. We were given a leather halter with about five feet of rope on it. We had to put this and our saddle on him, mount up and take the lariat off. The helper then went back to the chutes and we were on our own. The sorrel had a lot of fight. Mick and I both dug our heels in but he drug us about halfway across the arena before

Frank Robbins attempts to hobble Desert Dust. Palamino stallion corraled in the Red Desert with airplane.

we got him stopped. He swung around and faced us, Mick started up the rope towards him. He turned, and tried to run again, but both of us were able to hold him pretty good.

He faced us again. This time, it looked like he would hold his ground. Mick was just about up to him when he reared up and pawed the air. As he came back down, Mick made his move and grabbed him by an ear and twisted it. This took a lot of the fight out of him and I went for the halter and saddle. As I got near him with the saddle, I could see him tremble. He was a frightened horse and probably wondered what would happen next in his life of captivity.

My saddle went on fairly easy and I cinched it up good. He snorted plenty when I put the halter on, but the pressure Mick had on his ear kept him from bolting. My knees were shaking plenty when I stepped up on him, being real quick to get set.

Mick let go of the ear taking the lariat rope off at the same time. From then on it was just the stud and me. I spurred him in the shoulders. I knew this would make him buck and the people had paid to see a show. He bogged his head and humped up his back and really took to me, bucking in short quick jumps. This was a faster bucking horse than I had ever ridden and felt myself slipping a couple of times, but, somehow, managed to stay on top. He didn't buck very long and started running. The trick was to get him to run between two pick-up men who made up the finishing line. He ran to the far end of the arena at full speed. I hoped he would turn for the fence. He did turn and started back towards the other end. I couldn't do anything with him by pulling on the halter rope, so I began slapping him alongside the head with my hat.

I could turn him a little by using this method and after about three tries, I made it between the two riders. The next thing to think about was how to get off this running machine without getting hurt. Just as he got near the end of the arena he slowed down to turn, that is when I left him. This was no three point landing. I rolled like a sack of potatoes that had just fallen off a truck. Picking myself up, I took a quick look around. The arena seemed to be full of wild horses, some with riders on and some just running with empty saddles.

The sorrel had kept me so busy, I hadn't paid attention to what had taken place in the arena. Dave was still mounted and just getting his bronc hazed across the finish line. Dad and Mick were standing side by side in front of the chutes both grinning from ear to ear when I walked up. They congratulated me for winning first place. I had been so preoccupied, that I didn't realize I was first to cross the finish line.

Handshakes were in order and as I shook Mick's big, hairy hand, I realized what a powerful man he was. I said, "Thanks, Mick. I'm glad I had someone with guts and muscle on the front end of the horse." He just grinned and said, "We made him behave, didn't we pardner?"

After the rodeo, we split up with Frank. Dad sold some horses and traded a few around Rawlins. He ended up with a 1929 Model A Ford 2 door that we loaded our gear into. He fixed a bed in the back seat for both of us because it was getting cold at night. We headed our horses west along old Highway 30. This would be the shortest route back to Twelve Mile Spring and our camp. It took three days of hard pushing to get our herd back to camp. We arrived there just at sundown and there was a cold drizzle in the air. We found the big tent torn to a frazzle. The wind had evidently done a job on it. We slept in the Ford again that night. The next day we put up the smaller tent and began preparing it for a winter shelter. We picked a spot on the south side of a steep knoll. This would break the cold winds from the north and west.

The smaller tent was quite unhandy, compared to the bigger one. It was quite easy to bend over to pull your socks on, burn your bottom on the hot stove and tip the sugar bowl over on the table, almost simultaneously. A chain reaction like this was always good for a laugh.

We went right to work, setting out our trap lines. The coyote sign was plentiful. Tracks were visible in the mud at the spring where they had come to drink. If they were lucky they could possibly catch a water dog to eat.

The winter seemed to move slowly, as we routinely went about our daily work of trapping coyotes and badgers and breaking a few horses.

Don Ropes the Half & Half

We eagerly waited for the arrival of Spring so we could get back to building our wild horse corral. Upper most in our minds was the Half & Half. We hadn't seen that beautiful stallion all winter. He was probably over in the country between Coal Spring and Black Rock Butte. We hadn't been in that area with our trap lines. We had taken time to glass the area from the Ten Mile Rim several times and we could see several herds of mustangs. From this distance we could only tell they were horses. As soon as the frost had gone out of the ground, we were digging post holes and stringing cable and wire. Most of the main posts around the corral were braced with a dead man.

A dead man was a short piece of post or a large rock, buried in the ground about six feet from the post which needed the support. The hole was approximately four feet deep. The short post was laid horizontally, a long strand of #9 wire wound back and forth between it and the top of the post of the corral several times, then secured on both ends. The hole was then filled with dirt and tamped as solid as possible. A stick was then inserted between the strands of wire enabling the wire to be twisted. As it became twisted it became very tight, making it a very good guy wire.

By the time the corral was finished, the saddle horses had put in a good restful winter and spring so they were ready to go. We had fed them plenty of oats and had ridden them just enough to put them in top condition. We were now ready to capture the Half & Half horse.

Don and I took the field glasses and mounted up on The Candy Horse and Tippy. The early morning air was still a bit crisp and the horses pranced and pulled at the bit, wanting to run. We held them in check, for there would be plenty of running to do when we once started a wild herd of horses. Don and I visited as we rode. We were lucky to have Don home on furlough to help with the very first run to our new corral.

Dad, Sweed and Jean stayed in camp for awhile after Don and I left. They would take the day herd out to graze and have them in position in or near the wings of the corral, waiting for us to bring a herd of mustangs to be corralled.

We were especially looking for the Half & Half. Following a well used horse trail, we headed almost northwest from the camp. The trail led towards Black Rock Butte. As we approached the Coal Spring draw, we dismounted and cautiously peeked over the ridge into the draw in hopes we'd spot the stallion of our choice. Of the two herds we could see from the ridge, neither contained the Half & Half.

We stayed out of sight and continued on towards the head of the draw. We didn't want to spook the horses in the draw as they would probably run out of there, possibly spooking the herd we were intent upon finding. When we found the herd of mustangs dominated by the Half & Half, we wanted to be ready to approach them from the proper side, with the wind in our favor sending our human scent in the opposite direction. We also wanted to start them running towards the corral. We rode on for a couple of miles, nearing the sight where I had first seen this unusually marked horse. As we rode along a well used horse trail, Don spotted a lone horse in a little brushy draw. We kept on along the trail until we found a low place allowing us to be completely out of sight of the lone horse. There could easily be more horses in the draw, located at a lower level where they wouldn't be visible to us. After dismounting, we cautiously led our mounts towards a small knoll which would allow us to look down the draw without being in sight of the lone wild horse.

Our theory proved to be right. From our vantage point we could make out the Half & Half with about ten mares and several colts. Don rode around to position himself between the wild bunch and Black Rock Butte. He would start them. I stayed near where we had seen them from the knoll. I would try to keep them from running to Dead Man Canyon if they should decide to try that means of escape. After checking my cinch, I rolled my jacket up and tied it behind the cantle of my saddle. This wouldn't be needed once the running got under way. By this time I figured Don would be about ready to start them. Cautiously, I made my way back to the knoll for a look. What I saw didn't exactly please me. There were no horses in sight, but the long trail of dust hanging in the sage brush covered draw was an indication of horses running in the wrong direction. The next draw to the west had a shorter wisp of dust in it, kicked up by my brother's saddle horse, as he followed in hot pursuit. On a knoll was a buck antelope. He was whistling and acting very nervous. He had evidently gotten the scent of Don and with the fury of his investigation had spooked the horses.

The wild bunch headed due north, crossing the Black Rock wash just below the Butte. After crossing the wash, they took a northeasterly heading leading them towards the Sumps Of Alkali. The sumps were a series of lakes deep in the sand hills, caused by the sun beating down upon the dunes causing deeply buried snow to melt, slowly seeping to the lower ground, forming the series of lakes. These were excellent watering holes for all things living on the desert.

As the mustangs crossed the sands, I couldn't see any dust. They had evidently slowed down. Running in ankle deep sand makes for hard going, besides the sand doesn't cause as much dust to be kicked up as the loose dusty soil where sage brush grows.

As I watched through the field glasses, there were several bunches of mustangs grazing on the Buffalo Bench. That seemed the most likely place for the Half & Half to go with his tiring herd. The Bench is a wide flat area, beginning at the sand hills and gradually rising to the north. At the very edge of the north side is a high knoll, partly brush covered, resembling a buffalo's back. This is Buffalo Hump.

Don was visible again and was moving right out. Between him and the wild bunch, they were raising quite a dust cloud as they headed towards the horses on the Buffalo Bench. Don was soon out of sight, but all of the horses seemed to be running towards Buffalo Hump. I could only hope the Half & Half wouldn't get mixed up with all of these fresh horses. If that happened we would very likely lose the whole bunch.

Leading Tippy, I moved to a higher hill. From there I could see more of the desert floor, as well as having a better view of the Buffalo Bench area. From this vantage point I could see more dust and running horses, but from this distance, nothing looked clear to me and I had this fear that the Half & Half with his herd had gotten in with the fresh horses and Don had lost them. Bringing me out of this train of thought was a thin wisp of dust being kicked up by a horse and rider quite a ways east of where I had last seen Don. Soon the wild bunch came running out of the sand hills. Don had gotten around them and was bringing them back towards me. Excitement ran high within me as I realized the excitement of the chase would soon be mine.

The Half & Half led the herd, running easily about ten lengths ahead of the lead mare. The whole bunch was strung out, with the tail enders far behind. They were getting tired from the long run they'd already had. The stud kept coming at a fast clip when all of a sudden he almost whirled, making a ninety degree turn to the south. This left me on the wrong side of the ridge to help. Something had evidently spooked him, but I never did know what did it. All I could do is stay out of sight and follow along. Don continued on, hoping he could make them swing around enough to hit the day herd in the wings of the corral.

Don didn't crowd them and the mares and colts soon caught up to the stallion, continuing on up the ridge towards our corral. The bad part of it being, they were going to miss the wings of the corral. Dad, like me, had seen the chain of events too late to reposition himself and was unable to help.

By the time I reached the top of the ridge, the dust was thick in the canyon past the corral. Dad had ridden quickly out, spooking the day herd as he left, Jean and Sweed were having a hard time controlling it as I rode up to help them.

We corralled them for awhile, waiting for them to settle down before we turned them out to be held in the wings of the corral in case Don and Dad would be able to bring the wild horses back. We knew this wasn't too likely but we would be ready if they did. The sun was nearly down, with darkness quickly approaching, all we could do was wait. We watched the orange horizon until our eyes hurt. Finally we saw two riders with a lone horse between them. We knew they had one on a rope. We corralled the day herd again and waited to see what was on the rope. Just before it got too dark to see, they rode into camp. Don had roped the Half & Half.

We had finally captured that beautiful, notorious stallion. The stallion fought and pulled so much that Dad put a rope on him too. Don's Candy horse was about done in from the long continued chase and didn't need all of that hassle.

Dad had positioned himself slightly to the rear of the captured stud as they made their way to camp. This would keep the horse moving in a forward direction. He stopped once and Dad slapped him on the rump with the end of his lariat rope. The Half & Half immediately kicked Dad on the shin, cracking the shin bone. Dad wouldn't go to a doctor with it and hobbled around camp for quite awhile. Finally it festered up and a couple splinters of bone worked their way through the skin. This helped it to heal and brought much relief from the pain. I believe Dad carried a slight limp to his grave from the capture of the Half & Half.

It will always amaze me, how that little roan horse (Dick's Candy horse, or Kevroanie, as we called him) ever made that long run, carrying Don and still coming up with enough stamina to put him up close enough to rope the stud. Kevroanie is a name derived from a Spanish slang used by the Mexican hands to express displeasure with a dog or horse. We didn't use it that way, but with the horse being roan, the name just seemed to fit.

Don said he saved his horse as much as possible, not running him hard except to turn the wild bunch back from Buffalo Hump. He went at a trot or a slow lope, but just kept it up all day. He said the Half & Half was back and forth from the front to the rear of the herd, trying to keep them all together. He did this several times, putting on extra miles. This helped to wear him down too. Don said when he got his rope down Old Kevroani seemed to know which one they were after and dropped in behind the Half & Half, gradually closing up the gap until Don roped him.

Don's furlough had been too short to please all of us, I'm sure. We missed him as we had missed Short after he had been home. Chuck didn't get a furlough, but just before he shipped out for over seas duty, he came home AWOL. He told his platoon leader that he wasn't going over seas without seeing his Dad and brothers and sisters. He only spent about an hour with us at the horse camp, then had to run to get back to California to ship out. We received one letter after he returned to his outfit. He said he had to do KP for a few days for being AWOL but it was worth it. The next "and final" letter we received was a V mail letter in which he said they were floating around on the pond. The next word of Chuck was a telegram from the War Department. He had been in a black-out convoy and while driving a Jeep, he was in a head on collision with a two ton truck. This happened near Mesina, Italy. He is buried there in a military cemetery.

Horse Trading

As I lay there, one winter night, not very sleepy at that early hour, my mind wandered back to my boyhood days in South Dakota. My first recollection of my Dad's being a horse trader pertains to eating. (Food always was my weakness).

When Dad returned with his covered wagon, after being on the road for a couple of weeks of trading horses, we kids always got to raid his wagon and eat up the goodies he happened to have left. The two most popular items being peanut butter and Fig Newton cookies. These items kept well without being refrigerated. He had no ice box in the wagon. We also became familiar with canned milk through this horse-drawn home on wheels. Canned milk is not good the first time you taste it, but it eventually grows on you and soon it is delicious on oatmeal, in coffee to replace cream, or almost anyway you care to use it.

The first time I can remember going on the road with Dad was a big day in my life. He had nick-named me Jack The Horsetrader before I can remember and I always wanted to go with him trading horses. He told me, "when you get big enough, you can go with me." I was five years old and had already learned to ride our shetland pony, Jeff. On one of my first rides, Jeff started to trot with me and I fell, not just off, but directly under the old pony. Old Jeff stopped dead in his tracks and just stood there until I had gotten up. Dad was working near by and came over to see if I was hurt. I was shook up a little and scared but otherwise unhurt. As he lifted me up and put me back on, he explained, "If you get bucked off, you have to get right back on, otherwise the old pony will think he has you buffaloed and you will never be able to ride him again. This bolstered my courage as well as being soothing to my wounded dignity. Somehow it sounded better to say I got bucked off instead of just falling off.

On this day, as we pulled out of the yard, there was a feeling within me of having attained one goal in life, sort of gradu-

Melvin, Jack and Short by Dad's horse trading wagon. Note. White team of mules.

ation from being a little kid (I must have been all of five years old). As I sat upon the seat of the wagon, which was called the feed rack, alongside of my Dad and looked back at my cousin, Melvin Ball, who was driving the team of white mules hitched to the covered wagon, I knew this would be an adventure never to be forgotten.

We were living on a farm called the Hillstead place, located on the east bank of the Jim River at the time. As we pulled the hill leading northeast away from the building site, the harness tugs pulled tight as the teams labored under the load. When we crested the hill, the road leveled some as we left the river valley. The wagons pulled easier here allowing the metal chains at the ends of the heavy leather tugs to jingle in rhythm with the walking of the horses. My brothers, Chuck, Don and Short, came riding behind, herding about twenty head of bucking horses to eventually be used in a rodeo in Redfield that would be produced by Dad and Bill Maher. The trading stock was being led behind and alongside of the wagons. Some were hitched and were pulling the wagons. Actually, the horses were all trading stock. Horse traders always said, "I'll trade anything but my wife" and I'm sure they would have been tempted if somebody came along with the right kind of horse. They have been known to trade for anything of value and some things where the value was questionable.

Sundown found us pulling down a dirt two track road that obviously didn't get much use. After coming to a halt, Dad sent Mel to the east end of the mile of grass road with enough rope to tie across that end, while Chuck and Don did the same at the west end. The grass grew tall in this seldom used mile of country road, making it an excellent place to graze the horses. There was no water, but we had stopped a couple of miles back to water them at a farmer's stock watering tank. The next morning we would water them at Henry Albrecht's farm, which was just a mile away, directly across the section from where we were camped.

As the sun went behind the western horizon, the mosquitoes came up out of the tall grass by the thousands, resembling clouds. The horses began to fight them, by switching their tails, stomping their feet, rubbing together or any other way to rid themselves of the pesky insects. We were next to be picked as food for the hungry mosquitoes.

Dad said "a fire will help, the smoke will help to drive them away." He built a camp fire, using sticks from a dead tree which was near the camp. This probably did help keep the mosquitoes off, but the next thing Dad did was more beneficial to us by taking our minds off the mosquitoes for awhile.

Dad had entered the covered wagon, after much bumping and rattling of pots and pans, he emerged carrying a pop corn popper and a cup of popping corn. The popper was an oblong tin box with a sliding top made with screen so we could watch as the yellow kernels popped into huge white fluffy popped corn. The popper had a long handle and could be held over the open flame without burning the hands of the one holding it. The popper had to be shaken vigorously to keep the corn from burning on the bottom of the popper. It seemed to take quite a long time to start the actual popping process but once it began it sure wasn't long before the popper was full of the big white kernels pushing on the screen as if they were trying to get out.

Next, the corn was poured into a big bowl followed by melted butter which was poured over it. We all ate from the bowl after it had been salted to taste. This popcorn was a treat we kids hadn't counted on, but every now and then Dad would come up with a pleasant surprise to make life a little more enjoyable.

The next morning, after breakfast, we went to Henry Albrecht's farm. We didn't move the camp, but rode and herded the loose horses. After the horses had watered and Henry had looked them over, Melvin and my brothers took the loose horses back to the roped off road. Dad and I stayed at the farm. The summer before, Dad had traded Henry a big high spirited bay work horse. He knew the gray gelding Henry teamed him up with couldn't begin to keep up with him. he also knew Henry was an excellent horseman and teamster who enjoyed working horses who were evenly matched in their pulling and traveling abilities. He just figured Henry would be tired of having one arm longer than the other from holding the bay back even with the somewhat slower gray.

Dad was prepared, he had a big fiery brown to match the bay and he had a black, a much slower horse to match the gray gelding. Dad figured he could trade one of these horses to this farmer who he had traded horses with many times before.

Dad and Henry just sat and talked for a long time, nothing mentioned about horse trading, I was beginning to wonder if we had come all this way just to talk about the neighbors, the weather and the crops. The conversation finally worked it's way around to horses. Dad asked Henry if he had noticed the big bay gelding. Henry said he had. Dad continued, "he's a good honest horse, he'd make a good mate for the bay I traded you last year. He is a powerful horse with a fast walk. He could surely work abreast with the bay. If you like him, we will try to make a trade."

Henry was slow to answer, not wanting to show his eagerness to match his horse with one of equal caliber. He finally said "Jake, I have owned that gray horse for six years, in fact I raised him. His mother was a big gray mare, they don't come any better. His father was a black percheron that Leonard Hillestad used to travel. (Leonard used to lead the big stallion

I learned to ride on old Jeff, our shetland pony.

behind a pony cart from farm to farm servicing mares). The stallions were always well bred, if not pure bred horses.

Henry continued "He is a good honest work horse, gentle enough for anyone to work and handle, but he is too slow for the bay I got from you. I really don't want to get rid of him but if the black horse you have will work with him we'll try to make a trade. Two cups of coffee later, Dad and I mounted up and returned to the camp where Dad caught the black horse and returned to Henry's farm leading him to meet his new mate, the gray gelding. He would be there on a trial basis until we returned from Redfield.

We were on the road early the next morning. I had decided to ride in the covered wagon, with my pony tied on behind. We hadn't gone far when we heard a ruckus at the rear of the wagon. Mel stopped the team and we both went back to see what had caused the disturbance. The pony's lead rope had wound around the rear axle of the wagon, pulling his head down as if it were being winched. His nose had rubbed against the wheel taking the top layer of skin off. I felt bad about his sore nose which looked much worse than it was. Dad had noticed we were stopped and came back to find out what the hold up was. He smeared a bit of axle grease on the raw place to keep the flies off, and after tying the pony in a different place where the rope wouldn't wind around the axle, we were on our way again.

Our next stop was the Bruins farm, near Frankfort, Dad had known the Bruins for years and had traded horses with them many times. They had grown children who had left home to be on their own but Katie still lived at home. She was probably still in school. Hike and Albert lived on a farm south of Frankfort on the west bank of the Jim river. Ann was married to Bob Rawstern and lived near Hitchcock. Dad traded horses with all of them at one time or another. One of the Bruins boys had been riding on top of the threshing machine while it was being pulled to a different field. These machines, considered high in their day, were also top heavy, with the wheel base being quite narrow for the height of the large and cumbersome machine. The front wheels were also smaller than the rear wheels. As the Bruins moved the grain separator, one of the front wheels dropped into a hole, causing the machine to tip over, landing on the young man, killing him outright.

This accident had happened the summer before we were there but the tragedy was still present as it brought the tears in Mrs. Bruin's eyes as Mr. Bruins was telling us about the accident.

It was mid afternoon when we arrived at the Bruins farm. Dad had to deliver the rodeo horses to Redfield before dark so he decided to leave the teams, the wagons and horses, other than the rodeo stock, at the Bruins farm. He and the boys would have to ride hard to make it to Redfield by dark and it would be late in the night when they returned. He also decided to leave a very short cowboy who rode a very short legged pony behind too, as we wouldn't be able to keep up.

Not only did this damage my pride quite a lot, but I had never stayed away from home before and these people were all strangers to me. Katie took me in tow and we got along pretty well until she had to leave, probably had a date. That's when I pushed the panic button. I wanted to go to the covered wagon and go to bed. They wouldn't agree to that because they were supposed to watch me. This would require me to be in their sight, or at least in their house. I had a hard time believing this and started for the door but Mr. Bruins beat me to it and went out the door and held it shut. I was bawling and pushing to get out and he was holding me inside by keeping the door shut. After about twenty minutes, I gave up, retreating to a secluded spot behind the wood and coal burning kitchen range where I went to sleep. That's where Dad found me when he returned just after mid-night. I'm sure they had enough of taking care of me, and by the same token, I had enough of staying with strangers to last quite a spell. I can still remember that incident. It was a very frightening experience when he held the door on me. I believe to this day, it would have been better if he had taken me to the wagon and tucked me into bed.

The next day we all went to Redfield to help in preparation for the rodeo. Finishing touches had to be put on the bucking chutes. The crew had been working on the pens and chutes for several days. Everything had to be built from scratch and by hand. I doubt if there were any portable chutes and pens in 1930. The chutes were not "side delivery chutes" where the bucking animal comes out from the side of the chutes, as the modern day chutes are built. We had two long squeeze chutes each with a gate at the end where it entered the arena. This allowed one animal to be preparing for it's performance while the other was out in the arena performing.

It was hard to keep the show moving smoothly because many of the horses fought the chutes and everything around them, causing many delays. In those days the rodeo fans were used to this type of delay and took it very well.

My three older brothers rode steers and bare back broncs in this rodeo. My mother, my sisters and Sweed rode up to the rodeo with neighbors, so I went and sat with them during the rodeo. Dad was a pickup man, waiting until the saddle bronc riders had finished their eight second ride, to catch the horse's bucking rein, snubbing it to the saddle horn, allowing the rider to safely dismount.

Chuck rode a big old bull out of the chutes that day. That old bull had fought the chutes, trying to fight his way out of them. He was really mad, and adding to this fury was Chuck's spurring him in the shoulders. The old bull was strong and hit the ground hard when he came down. This jarred Chuck loose, tossing him over the head of the bull. As he was going over, the old bull tossed his head connecting one of his nubby horns with Chuck's forehead. Chuck landed in the dust of the arena, face down and didn't move. My mother would have been there if she could have gotten across the arena fence. He surely looked like he was badly hurt but Dad and another man carried him over to the shade of the chutes. He soon came to, not suffering much except a bad headache.

As a boy of five, I was impressed by several Indian families who had come to participate in the rodeo. Several of the men rode in the rodeo and they all did traditional dances in their very colorful native costumes. They had been furnished a steer to butcher, much of which they sliced very thinly and had hanging in the sun to dry. They made excellent jerky.

The day after the rodeo, we were up early, preparing for our trip back home. The horses had all been put into a small pasture near town, and we had to separate our horses from Bill's. This didn't take long, we were on the road by mid morning, heading for Henry Albrecht's farm again.

Henry was working in the field when we arrived in his yard. He had been watching for us and soon arrived at the gate with his four horse team. By the time the horses had watered at the stock tank, Dad was at Henry's side asking how the black had worked out for him. Again Henry spoke slowly, not wanting to show his eagerness. Quite often the asking price of a horse was based upon how badly the purchaser wanted the animal. These old seasoned horse traders were aware of this so they kind of jockeyed for the best bargaining position. Henry replied "Jake, I like the horse but he isn't quite as tall as my gray. They do work good together and he gets along well with my horses, I'll trade even up." Dad came aback with "I'll have to have ten to boot, the black cost me more than the bay did." They finally split the difference and a horse trade was completed.

The next trade to be made was at the Bill Marquardt farm which was located near Cottonwood Lake. We had a bay stallion hitched to the feed rack alongside the bay gelding we had just received back from Henry Albrecht. This stud was a mild mannered horse as long as he was around horses familiar to him, but around strange horses, he was a typical stallion, prancing, whinnying and acting up. He had plenty of pep, a sleek coat of hair and was big enough to pull his share of the load.

This horse had caught Bill's eye as we drove up the driveway leading to his farm. He came out into the yard as we came to a halt near the watering tank. He slowly eyed the horses as he circled the outfit. Coming to a halt near the bay stud's head, he proceeded to mouth the horse. The teeth showed him to be seven years old. "Just in the prime of this life" Dad said, "What will you give for him?" He replied, "I have a little black saddle horse in the barn. The Gypsies traded him to me when they went through early this Spring. He is pretty as a picture but you have to watch him. If he doesn't get ridden regularly, he might buck.

The black was brought out of the barn where my brother, Chuck, put a saddle on him. He was indeed a pretty horse with two stocking feet behind and a star in his forehead. As Chuck pulled the cinch tight, the old pony humped up his back and began jumping around stiff legged. It was quite obvious this horse wouldn't be ridden without a fight. Dad held the reins up tight while Chuck climbed aboard. That little horse really came unglued until the buck was out of him. The horse, realizing he had met his match, settled down nicely, proving himself to be well broke to neck-reining and performing to the rider's commands. He had obviously bucked a few people off and wouldn't give up trying very easily. Dad said, "I'll take twenty dollars to boot." Bill readily agreed, obviously being completely buffaloed by the fiery little outlaw.

The next bit of excitement came when Bill took the horse he had just traded for and turned him in his pasture. He took off with head and tail in the air, letting out a big squeal as he headed out on the run to meet the strange horses. Bill was speechless for awhile, then he said "jeeeeez, Jake, I didn't know it was a stud. Will you take him back? But I don't want the black horse back, do you have another one you will trade? Dad offered the other bay that we had driven with the stud, but said he'd have to have another ten dollars to boot. Bill said he was a little hard pressed for cash, but would throw in a calf on the trade. He had lost a cow to sweet clover bloat, orphaning a calf.

We milked cows at home and would be able to care for it. It surely wasn't unusual for farmers to be hard up for cash in 1930. Times were tough, with farm commodities selling for very little money. Chuck was sent out, riding the black, to bring Bill's horses up to the place so we could retrieve the bay stud. The bay was chasing, fighting and in general raising havoc with the other horses. Bill couldn't wait to get him out of his herd. The calf was loaded into the feed rack, which was now being hitched to the team of white mules we had been leading behind the feed rack. Once again the wagons rolled towards the James River and the corrals of the Price place.

The little black horse we traded Marquardt out of, continued to love to buck, making him a willing candidate for the bucking string where he made quite a reputation for himself.

Of all the horse trading my Dad did, he didn't get beat very often, but one little sorrel and white pony comes to mind. This little horse was as pretty as any you'd care to lay eyes on. I got home from school just as Dad was unloading him from the truck. He was such a keen looking little horse that I just knew he would be a perfect pony for us kids to ride. Dad put the bridle on him and gave me a boost up onto his back. The pony was an easy rider, reined like a good little cow pony, was eager to go so I rode him until dark. After tying him in the barn, I went into the house to report upon what a good pony he was.

The next morning I was up extra early, allowing myself enough time to have a good ride on him before it was time for me to head off to school. After bridling the pony, I tried to lead him out of the stall. He wouldn't budge. I pulled and pulled on the reins. I slapped him on the rump with the reins but he still didn't take a step. Dad was milking cows in the cow barn so I got him to help me. We thought the old pony was playing opossum and didn't want to be ridden. Dad took the reins and attempted to lead him. Still no action, it was as if he was glued to the floor of the barn. Dad took one of his front feet in his hand, moving it ahead, then the other. We finally got him turned around and out of the barn. Dad said he probably had rheumatism or arthritis, causing him to be stiffened up after standing in the stall over night. After he was limbered up and warmed up, he was back to normal. We kept him in a box stall after that, so he wouldn't have to be kept tied up. We didn't keep him very long. He was made trading stock, probably ended up in a glue factory. I felt bad to see him go. He was such a pretty thing and so easy to ride.

Dad had traded for a team of buckskin mules, well matched for color, size and pulling ability. They were small, trim built and pretty as a picture. One sunny afternoon, when he was away from home, the older boys decided to find out if they were broke to ride. It seems like a lot of these things just happened to take place when Dad was gone. They had one mule caught and were trying to decide whether to saddle him or ride him with a loose rope, when Don said, "I'll ride him with a mane hold." The mule was gentle, cooperating very well until about the time Don got straddle of him, then he came uncorked, losing Don on about the fifth jump. The little mule was startled to say the least and when he saw Don falling alongside of him, he just had to kick him, because that is what mules are famous for. He connected with my brother about in the mid section, really knocking the wind out of him.

I just knew he was dead and hurried to the house to inform Mamma. By the time I arrived back at the corral with Mamma hot on my heels, Don was up and they were debating about trying the other mule. Mother took all of the guess work out of that decision when she said, "There will be no more bronc riding around here when your Dad isn't home."

The three older boys picked up the air rifle and headed down towards the river. I went in the other direction, into the grove of trees, more or less as a refuge. I had caught a couple of quick glances from Chuck and Don, which gave me the impression they weren't too pleased with me for running to mamma with the news of Don's being knocked out by the buckskin mule. I normally didn't tattle on my big brothers. They had taken that out of me early on, but this time I was so sure Don was dead or at least hurt bad, that I panicked. With that exciting episode still on my mind, I drifted off to sleep.

The Coyote Den

While going hell bent for leather, chasing a wild bunch of mustangs, I spotted a coyote den about five miles from our camp. The bitch coyote was just leaving the hole and wasted no time in getting away from it. She had probably been in to feed her pups. Glancing over my shoulder, I picked out two sandy knolls as reference landmarks. Sweed and I would go back and dig the pups out next day as we seldom ran horses two days in a row. We were lucky to corral the horses I was after just as darkness was upon us.

As we ate our late supper, I told Dad and Sweed about the den and my plan to dig them out. Dad said with the newly captured horses, we would probably be tied up all fore noon, with the branding and then putting them with the day herd. He said if it got too late, I could go the next morning, but Sweed would have to help with the day herd.

We were practically all day, branding, castrating the stallions and getting them adapted to the day herd. The next morning we were up early. I wrangled the saddle horses while Dad prepared breakfast. Right after we had eaten, we put the day herd out to graze. As soon as it looked as if the new horses would stay with the day herd, I left to dig out the coyote den. The task of finding the den wasn't quite as simple as I had anticipated. There were more of the sandy knolls than I had figured to deal with. The first two were definitely not the ones. There was no hole between them and no fresh tracks to indicate my passing there two days before. Riding farther east with my eyes to the ground, tracks were visible where the mustangs had passed this way on the run. I had been east of the horses when the den was spotted, so I kept riding east. The next two knolls proved to be the pair with the den between them. I had ridden Old Billy, a horse we had bought from Bill Adkins from the Black Willow Mink Ranch of Coalville Utah. This ranch bought our cripples and old horses. Occasionally Bill would

bring us a horse somebody had sold for mink feed. The horses
he brought to us were too good for slaughter and we always
needed saddle horses which were mature and ready to go. We
got several good horses from him, plus a few which were not
so good. We never did send any of them back to be slaugh-
tered. Old Billy was one of these horses. He was a little on the
lazy side, really didn't have much speed, but was a very gentle
and dependable old pony. The latter is why I chose to ride him
to dig out the coyotes. I knew he wouldn't throw a fit if I hung
a sack on each side of him, which contained coyote pups. After
tying Old Billie to a large sage bush, I began to dig. The hole
went in and downward at about a 20 degree angle. I began to
tunnel, just enlarging the hole enough to allow me to enter. As
the tunnel progressed, and I made my way into the den, my
imagination ran amock, as it sometimes did at this time of my
life. Right at the moment, I didn't know if I should feel like an
old dog coyote returning to the den to visit my family, or if I
should be an intruder, which in fact I was. What if the old
mother was still with the pups, deep within the deep hole in
the ground. She certainly wouldn't welcome me with a wag-
ging tail. As the digging continued, I began making noise, hoping to get some indication as to whether there was an adult
coyote in the den. No noises were forth coming. Tunneling my
way around a bend made me wish for a flash light. The lighting
made it almost impossible for me to see. While lying there,
contemplating going back to camp for a light, the realization
struck me. If the old mother coyote was in the hole, or if she
would return, to discover some intruder had violated her den,
she would surely have the pups removed before I could return.
Just as I had decided to abandon the whole venture, there was
a sound, made by something moving, just beyond the bend in
the tunnel. Remaining motionless, and watching closely soon
paid off in the form of two little shiny eyes looking at me, barely detectable in the dimly lighted hole. I grabbed for the pup
with my gloved right hand, catching it by one front foot. The
pup began to bite and howl. Lucky for me, I had heavy weight
leather gloves on. Getting out of the hole, crawling backwards
was quite an effort. The slight incline with the dirt loose from

the digging made it real hard going. As I backed out into the open, the light seemed extremely bright, causing me to squint my eyes until they became accustomed to the change. After putting the male pup into one of the burlap bags, I grabbed the other bag. Returning to the den, crawling on my belly, I made my way to where the first pup had been picked up. Going beyond the bend with just feeling with my hands to guide my way, another furry pup was found. He also put up quite a scrap. After putting it into the bag and tying it shut as best I could in the dark and cramped quarters, I began to feel, in search of any more pups which might be there. There was a good sized cavity here, indicating, this was the den. After feeling around and finding no holes or tunnels leading off from this main den, I was able to turn around, pick up my shovel along with the pup in the bag and return to day light in a much easier fashion than the first trip. The two bags, containing the coyote pups, were tied together and placed on the back of my saddle with one on either side of the gentle horse. I secured them, using the saddle strings to tie them in place. After mounting up, with the shovel over my shoulder, I started back to camp, going slowly so the pups wouldn't get shook up too much. I had hoped there would be more pups in the den, but apparently this was all she had. To break the monotony of the five mile trek back to the horse camp, I began to whistle a little tune. This little tune soon became intermittently broken up by my scratching an itchy neck. The itchy, and sometimes, crawly feeling made it's way right up under my hat band and into my hair, causing me to have to scratch my head to relieve the itching. Upon my arrival at camp, I told Dad about the itching. He looked and soon discovered I had been infested with mites, either from the coyote pups, or from inside the den. He washed my head with Grandpa's Pine Tar soap, adding a few drops of Creosote dip to the water. This sure did away with the mites and the itching. Nobody hung around me very close for a few days either, because of the odor of the Pine Tar soap and the dip which was normally used as a disinfectant on livestock.

We made a make-shift pen to put the pups in for the night and darkness was soon upon us. The next morning one of the pups was gone. We couldn't figure out how one could get out without the other one following, but it sure enough did. The remaining one was a male. We named him Smokey. Dad said he probably wouldn't tame very much. He said if they are caught before their eyes are open they tame quite easily. These pups had definitely had theirs open for several days. We put a collar on him, tying him with about twenty feet of dog chain, allowing him to play along a ledge of rocks which included a hollowed out place. This made an excellent place for him to sleep and to get out of the weather.

Dad was sure right about his not getting tame. We had him for about two months, hand feeding him every day. We couldn't get near him unless we pulled him to us with the chain. As we pulled him, the closer he got to us, the more ferocious he would become, snapping at us as he tried to pull away.

Dad was in Point Of Rocks one day telling the gas station owner about the pup. The guy said he would like to have him in a pen as an attraction for motorists as they gassed up their vehicles at his station. On our next trip to town, we left Smokey to become a tourist attraction at Point Of Rocks, Wyoming.

I have a thought about this venture so often, and the seriousness of it, had the soft and sandy soil of the den in the hillside caved in while I was digging in there so far that my feet wouldn't have been visible. I guess luck was with me that time again.

Shipping Out

The heat of the desert summer was bearing down on us as we worked with the horses we had in the day herd. I was breaking five head to the saddle and we had five of the best yearlings tied up, halter breaking them. The nights cooled off real good and the moon shined almost as bright as day, lighting up the whole countryside. Dad and I were setting in front of the tent in silence. Neither of us was great at talking, but we professed to be deep thinkers. We could hear horses on the trail and could see a large herd on the trail, headed for the spring to drink of the clear cool water. The old desert had become so dry, they had to come to the spring to drink. We just sat there quietly until they left. Dad said if it was that light the next night, we would be saddled up and waiting. We would rope a couple. It sounded like an excellent idea to me. a little chill swept through me as I thought about the excitement.

The next day was hot. We didn't do much except graze the day herd and take care of the ones we had tied up. Just after sundown we saddled our best roping horses. Dad would ride Shorty, and I saddled Tippy.

We waited in the washout above the spring. The slight breeze from the north was in our favor. They wouldn't smell us if they came in from the same direction that they had the night before.

The moon was full and really giving off her fullest light as we waited for the first sign of wild horses to show up at the water hole. First to show up was a nice herd of antelope. They came in from the south and smelled us and there was a lot of whistling and stomping of feet, but they finally had their drink of water and went on their way.

After what seemed like many hours, the horses showed up. We let them take on a good fill of water. Then after a reassuring pat on the neck for my mount, I stepped into the saddle and rode slowly towards the spring. Dad did the same. He swung to the right, and I to the left, of the wild bunch. They soon saw us

176

and one of them, probably the stud, gave a shrill whistle and the race was on.

Tippy ran good and I was sure I could rope the stud because he was full of water. We gained real good on him, but about two-thirds of the way to the top of the ridge, my sight was gone. Dust had settled in from all of the running hooves and I couldn't see past the end of my nose. There were horses running on all sides of me. I could hear them, and once in a while see a shape, but my only thought now was for survival. My horse might step in a hole or stumble on a rock. The flat rocks clattered as we crossed the ridge. Not daring to pull up and stop, because I would get run into from behind, I gradually pulled to the left until I could see again.

Dad came riding up shortly. He, too, had been blinded by the dust and quit. We had a good chuckle on the way back to camp, but both admitted that it was pretty scary, riding at top speed in the middle of a herd of wild horses, when you couldn't see anything.

As the summer progressed, it continued to be hot and dry. Horses had to come to the Twelve Mile spring to drink from far away. Several bunches watered in the daylight because they didn't know the corral was there or that we were camped nearby.

One day, Sweed and I were saddled up and waiting as a nice herd of sleek mustangs came slowly down the dusty trail. They made their way cautiously to the spring of cold, clear water and took on a good fill. Just as they were leaving the draw, we jumped them. They went right out on the wagon road that lead out towards Black Rock Butte. We fell right on behind them, one of us in each track. Sweed was riding Lady, the little bay mare. She was really fast, and with a light rider on her back, could outrun Tippy, who I was riding. We passed about one-half of the horses thinking I might get a chance to rope the stud. My younger brother probably could have caught him but he had a real light saddle and couldn't rope off it. Finally, deciding that I wouldn't catch the stud, I singled out a nice bay mare. As I slowly got closer to her, hoping to catch her on the first throw, Sweed was cheering me on yelling, "Hang it on her Jack! Hang it on her!."

When I was about a length and a half behind her, I swung my loop. On the third swing, I let drive with all my strength. The loop settled nicely over her head. Just as soon as she hit the end of the rope, she started squalling and bellering, rearing and pawing the air. She was a real fighter. she finally decided she wasn't getting anyplace by fighting, and settled down as we hazed her back to the corral.

Dad had made a couple of trips back to South Dakota to visit Grandma Price, who was getting along in years, and seemed to be failing in health. Dad said South Dakota looked real good as it had been getting plenty of rain. The grass was tall and farmers were raising good crops again. He had decided that we should move back to be with Grandma, but we would return to Wyoming after the war, when we had all of our hands together. We would build a big corral in the Red Desert and catch many more mustangs. We would ship a rail car load of our best horses to South Dakota where the market for saddle horses was real good at that time.

Sweed and I trailed the horses to the stock yards at Point of Rocks. Dad and Jean took the Model A to Superior to load up what we would take along. It was nearly sundown by the time we got to the stock yards.

We had only been there about ten minutes when the first Union Pacific freight train rolled past at a fast clip. The smoke was rolling out of the stack of the old steamer and the engineer was really laying on the whistle. Boy! You talk about a scared bunch of horses; we sure had them. Most of these had never seen a train before. I was glad we had gotten them inside the pens before any train came along. They would have ran every direction and we surely would have lost some of them.

Sun-up the next morning found us loading the horses into the car. We led old Pappy in first (he wasn't afraid of anything), and drove the rest in after him. The last one to go up the chute was the Half & Half. Just before he entered the car he stopped, looked back with a longing look towards the desert, then followed the others into the car.

We quickly rolled the big door shut, not realizing at the time, that we were closing the door on our last wild horse escapade.

About the Author

Jack Price rode in his first rodeo at Lake Campbell near Brookings, South Dakota, at age 10. He started out riding calves. It wasn't until the following summer that he tackled a big Brahma. The bull bucked him down as if he were a fly, but this didn't discourage the young cowboy from riding.

His father, Jake Price, moved his family to Wyoming when Jack was 12 years old. Jake and his five sons became involved in running and corralling wild horses in Fire Hole and on the Red Desert. Eventually, they worked with Frank "Wild Horse" Robbins.

Jack Price

After World War II, Jack farmed for 10 years and then drove a gasoline transport for 21 years. He is now retired and lives with his wife, Mavis in Wolsey, South Dakota. Jack is active in the campaign to preserve the wild mustang.